RED, WHITE, & BOLD
THE NEW AMERICAN CENTURY

"*Delfeld's conservative blueprint to renew America's prosperity is right on the money.*"

—Larry Kudlow
Host of CNBC's
"Kudlow & Company"

RED, WHITE, & BOLD
THE NEW AMERICAN CENTURY

CARL T. DELFELD
Forbes Asia Columnist
AmericaUnbound.org

iUniverse, Inc.
New York   Bloomington

iUniverse books may be ordered through booksellers or by contacting:

iUniverse
1663 Liberty Drive
Bloomington, IN 47403
www.iuniverse.com
1-800-Authors (1-800-288-4677)

Because of the dynamic nature of the Internet, any Web addresses or links contained in this book may have changed since publication and may no longer be valid. The views expressed in this work are solely those of the author and do not necessarily reflect the views of the publisher, and the publisher hereby disclaims any responsibility for them.

ISBN: 978-1-4401-5130-9 (sc)
ISBN: 978-1-4401-5131-6 (dj)
ISBN: 978-1-4401-5129-3 (ebook)

Printed in the United States of America

iUniverse rev. date: 08/05/09

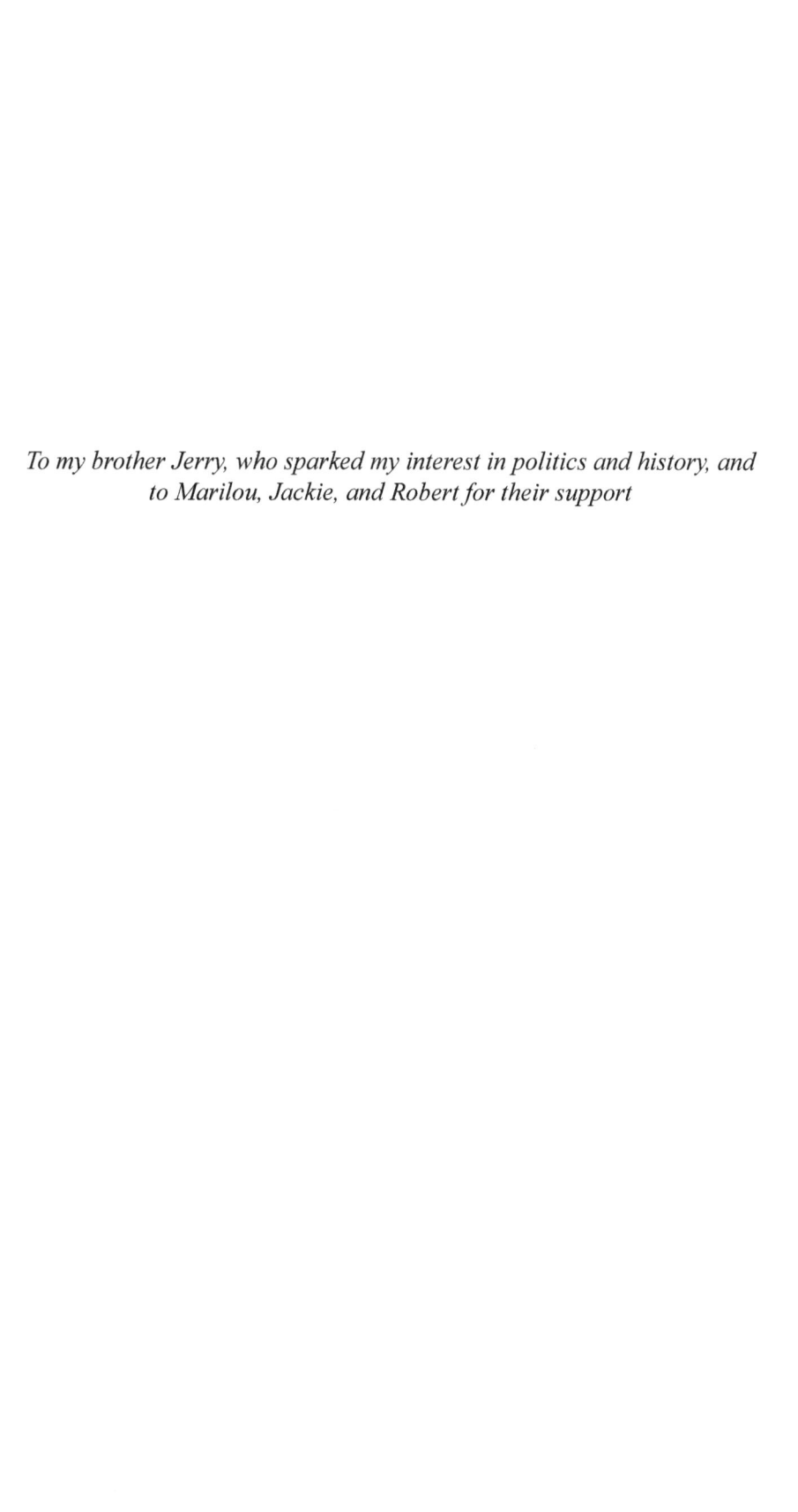

To my brother Jerry, who sparked my interest in politics and history, and to Marilou, Jackie, and Robert for their support

Also by Carl Delfeld

Think Global, Grow Rich

The New Global Investor

ETF Investing Around the World

Passport to Profits

"Our future is in our hands. But our hands must be strong, nimble, and confident for history shows that great countries and civilizations often fail due to one or more of three shortcomings: a lack of fiscal discipline; a culture that does not promote risk taking, openness, scientific innovation, or the common good; and a foreign policy not grounded in the national interest and executed at the extremes of isolationism or foreign interventionism."

—The Author

"One thing seems probable to me: The United States will lose its status as the superpower of the global financial system."

—Peer Steinbruck
German Finance Minister

"More people understand that America is not as great as it was ten years ago. This is not a time for China to be on a par with America. But the relative shift of the center of gravity does bring China more confidence."

—Shen Dingli
Fudan University

"Pan Wei, director of the Center for Chinese and Global Affairs at Beijing University, mused aloud to me that 'my belief is that in twenty years we will look the Americans straight in the eye—as equals. But maybe it will come sooner than that. Their system is in chaos and they need our money to rescue them."

—Financial Times,
September 29, 2008

"And I confess that, notwithstanding Tuesday's great events [Obama's inauguration], I also continue to brood over the near-inevitable decline of the United States as the world's top power, and what that means for those who hold most of their wealth here."

—Nadav Manham
President, Elera Advisors LLC

"The era of Western domination has run its course."

—Kishore Mahbubani
The New Asian Hemisphere

Table of Contents

Introduction

Why It Matters

The United States is not just another country.

America has been a rich country from the very beginning. Hessian mercenaries were startled by the standard of living they encountered as they marched to Manhattan to put down the American rebels. After the Americans emerged victorious, fully one third of the Hessians decided to make America their new home.

America is a nation with a "why not?" attitude and represents a land of second chances. Deep in the DNA of America is the ambition for success and the drive to stay first among equals. Why does it matter that it stays this way?

It matters because America is the world's last best hope, a force of good in the world, first among equals, and an indispensable source of progress, discovery, and growth. Benjamin Franklin echoed this sentiment when he stated that the "cause of America is the cause of all mankind." American values are

Western values, and we still set the clock of the political and commercial world.

This is clear to me not in spite of my professional specialty in Asia and emerging markets, but rather because of it. As a financial publisher, the author of four books on global investing, and columnist for *Forbes Asia*, I follow global economics and finance closely. Through my experience covering Asia-Pacific markets for First Boston and Robert Baird, my stints with the U.S. Treasury and in the U.S. Congress, and my presence at the liftoff of a rising Asia when representing America on the executive board of directors of the Asian Development Bank, I have the perspective to evaluate America's challengers.

Without question, this can and should be a new American century.

But is this the attitude that most Americans have about their country right now? Polls show quite the contrary. The message is decidedly negative, dwelling on our nation's past mistakes and shortcomings and our economic and social problems. At risk is the belief that America's tomorrow will be better than today.

My guiding light in writing this book is to strengthen America's role as the world's leader. By this I mean the most prosperous nation, the strongest and most independent nation, and the most respected and influential nation.

This book is a blueprint to finding our way forward and getting back on track. It starts by highlighting ten reasons why America has become "first among equals" and the leader of the world. This means going beyond the dry and shopworn statistics to get at the "guts" of America's strength and resiliency

Next, it examines the threats to America's prosperity and challenges to our leadership. We face growing economic competition from Europe and other emerging nations, such as India and China, but our biggest threat to staying on top of the world is ourselves.

Then we turn to how to navigate back to growth and prosperity and fulfilling the promise of our Founding Fathers. Learn why it is absolutely essential to avoid the missteps of Japan, following its real estate bubble and financial meltdown. One lesson is that we should not follow the path of more government spending, higher taxes, and more regulation and red tape. Then we need to emulate and appreciate the values and principles of great leaders like George Washington, Abraham Lincoln, and Alexander Hamilton. They gave us the blueprint of self-reliance; independence; opportunity for advancement, discovery, and exploration; openness; and unity—as Thomas Jefferson put it, "a government small and frugal." Now we just have to follow it.

Finally, we end with a "why not?" agenda that will without doubt lead to a new American century and will transform the world into a better place. Our future is in our hands, and it is an unbounded future full of opportunity and hope. Americans should be proud of its country's past, appreciate its current strengths, and step confidently into its best future.

If you are looking for a much more positive view of America's past, present, and future—this book is for you. The current economic downturn is but a bump in the road to another American century that will make the twentieth century look like a warm-up for the big event. Volatility and swings in financial markets are nothing new, since to some degree they are as inevitable as fluctuating human emotions. There were six sharp economic downturns in the nineteenth century. Walter Armstrong, the former chairman of Princeton Economics, calculates that there were twenty-six financial panics between 1683 and 1907.

Most discussions highlighting America's hegemony in the world dwell on statistics, such as America representing about 25 percent of global economic output. More than a third of the world's largest companies are American, and 60 percent of the world's reserve currencies are held in U.S. dollars. Our defense expenditures are equal to roughly half of world defense spending and ten times that of the United Kingdom's defense budget. Our geographic and demographic advantages as well as our technological prowess are also often cited. These are all indeed impressive, but we need to dig a bit deeper to get at the true foundation of America's greatness.

These key advantages cannot be captured by mere economic statistics, for they are essentially ideas with great power and impact. As Winston Churchill once said, "America is an idea, not a place."

Here are just some of these ideas:

Our political freedoms and system; our unique culture of second chances; our educational opportunities second to none; our tradition of philanthropy, volunteerism, and service; our foreign policy based on more than our narrow self-interest; our embracing of new ideas and technologies; our openness to legal immigration; and our acceptance of unequal outcomes. We have also made tremendous progress moving to a color-blind society and lead the world in such areas as the ease of starting a new business, respect for property rights, free press, due process and an independent judiciary, devotion to conserving our natural resources, love of the outdoors and competitive sports, belief in economic mobility, and achievement based on merit.

America can lengthen its lead if it boldly doubles down on its commitment to deepening these winning traits.

These traits are often unappreciated even by many Americans—but they underpin our economy and society and are vital to making what America is: the leader and envy of the world, the best hope of mankind. These traits embody the "why not?" attitude that drives our growth and prosperity.

The opportunity to be whatever one wants to be no matter how humble one's origins is one of the secrets of America—our "ace in the hole," in poker terms. In many countries, a person's future is narrowly cast by their circumstances of birth. In some countries, a humble beginning can be overcome by exceptional academic achievement, but by one's late teens, the die is cast.

Contrast this with the powerful story of Alexander Hamilton, born in the West Indies, fatherless with a mother who died while he was just a young boy. Hamilton rose to be General Washington's aide-de-camp during the Revolution and then our first and finest secretary of treasury and the architect of the modern American economy.

My hope is that you will find this book interesting and that it rekindles your appreciation for all the qualities and opportunities that America offers each and every one of us.

Let's get started by looking at why America is first among equals and how we can outcompete emerging nations like China and avoid some of the mistakes of Japan, as well as the unfortunate path that Europe has taken. We will end with a look back in American history for lessons to guide us to a "why not?" agenda to strengthen our prosperity and leadership.

There are many themes in this book that will help a Republican party that may appear to have shot its bolt recover its principles and promise. But whether you are a Republican, a like-minded Democrat, or a discerning independent, keep an open mind and read this book with a forward-looking attitude, for as Winston Churchill put it:

"If we open a quarrel between the present and the past, we shall be in danger of losing the future."

Carl T. Delfeld

Part One

Why America Is "First Among Equals"

America is a special country. Of course, in the eyes of God, all people are equal, and individual Americans are certainly no better than citizens of other nations. Rather, it is as a country that America is first among equals.

America has reached this stature in the world not by chance but rather by overcoming the stiffest challenges by always asking, "Why not?" It started when the Winthrops, Dudleys, Bradstreets, and the other colonists boarded the *Arbella* and improbably crossed the Atlantic to a new world. Full of faith, courage, and optimism, they asked themselves, "Why not?" and began the American saga.

George Washington, having never commanded more than a militia regiment, was offered the leadership of a ragtag army up against the most powerful military in the history of the world, not to mention risking his own economic ruin; he thought, "Why not?"

Abraham Lincoln, one-term congressman and twice a failed Senate candidate, saw a slim chance at gaining the presidency in a divided country; he thought, "Why not?" and went on to vindicate the Union and end slavery.

Undaunted by the incredible challenge of building a transcontinental railroad through the Rocky Mountains, the country asked, "Why not?"

Mounting the costliest, largest engineering challenge on Earth to build a canal to unite two great oceans, the country asked, "Why not?"

Faced with the daunting logistics of fighting World War II across the Atlantic and Pacific oceans at the same time, the country asked, "Why not?"

America, burdened by a crushing debt and exhausted by a world war, was immediately presented with the challenges of rebuilding Europe, bringing democracy to Japan, and containing the Soviet Union while expanding economic growth at home; the country thought, "Why not?"

Despite formidable and dangerous obstacles, millions of pioneer families crossed the prairies to build new lives in the wilderness; they thought, "Why not?"

Resisting the temptation to leverage its power to monopolize world markets, America instead asked, "Why not?" and expanded opportunities, opened markets, and spread liberty and capitalism.

But as I write these words, America seems anything but first among equals, having temporarily lost this precious "why not?" attitude. We are being humbled and challenged like never before in our nation's history. This may actually be a blessing in disguise, for humility is an essential ingredient for greatness in a person as well as a nation.

Our financial institutions are broken; though staging a partial recovery, our markets remain fragile; blue chip financial companies have either disappeared or have gone hat in hand for government bailouts; and consumers seem shell-shocked by economic uncertainty. Americans have suffered more than $15 trillion of losses to their home equity, retirement assets, and savings during 2008. Three out of four Americans believe the country is on the wrong track, we have wars in Iraq and Afghanistan, the mortgage and financial markets are in turmoil, and there is a steady drumbeat of negative news from the media; stating emphatically that America is the greatest may seem a bit quaint and out of touch.

Everyone seems to be in line for some sort of a bailout. While at the gym recently, my jaw dropped when I saw a clip of Governor Arnold Schwarzenegger, hat in hand, asking for a bailout for California. This, from the land of milk and honey which, if a country, would have the world's seventh-largest gross domestic product (GDP)? This from our preeminent action hero, the terminator?

America now seems to be a giant bound up by a rope made up of the strands of complexity, debt, taxes, red tape, rights without responsibilities, dependence rather than self-reliance, and most of all, an attitude of self-doubt and uncertainty rather than faith and confidence.

Clearly, America needs a big dose of reform and the "can do" attitude that led to the American century. David Reynolds in *Waking Giant* notes that the most common slang expression in mid-nineteenth century America was "Go ahead."

Americans are always looking ahead, fueled by pride in the past and hope for the future.

This book looks back at all we have accomplished as a people and nation, and then, more importantly, lays out, an aggressive "why not?" agenda for renewing America's greatness. After all, a trait of Americans is a willingness to learn and to strive to improve, knowing that complacency is a cardinal sin. We have always been inveterate tinkerers and inventors searching for a better way forward.

But does America have the confidence and courage that is worth more than money and gold? Does America still represent boundless optimism and limitless opportunities? Many might also ask; Does it even matter if America is leader of the world and continues its perpetual and limitless advance?

> Americans are always looking ahead, fueled by pride in the past and hope for the future.

The answer to this comes from Sir Winston Churchill in his "If I Were an American," essay published in *Life* more than sixty years ago:.

> When I reflected on the strengths of the United States, its freedoms and its many virtues, all the toils, sacrifices, costs, and burdens cast upon it, I might well have come to the conclusion that the United States has no choice but to lead or fail....

Americans should not hesitate to march forward unswervingly upon the path to which Destiny has called them, guided by the principles of the Declaration of Independence, expressed so carefully and so pregnantly in the balanced well-shaped language of the eighteenth century, by the founders of the greatest State in the world.

Still, a growing number of commentators insist that America is moving past the pinnacle of its economic power and global influence and that the twenty-first century belongs to Asia.

In Thomas Friedman's *The World Is Flat*, it is argued that because of breakthroughs in technology and communications, distinctions between countries are becoming less important. Fareed Zakaria's *The Post-American World* focuses on the rise of our competitors and the relative decline of American influence.

I believe that the world is round and that America is at the top. Even better, if we take vigorous action for the common good, America's best days are yet to come. We are still on the rise, way short of our apogee, with ample opportunities to expand our influence and prosperity.

As head of a financial publishing and investment advisory firm focused on global markets, I follow with keen interest the economic progress that many emerging market countries are making and applaud that a billion people have been pulled out of poverty over the last twenty years. Though the economic challenge from a rising Asia should not be underestimated, I also recognize many of the shortcomings of our competitors and believe the media is overstating America's weaknesses and missing many of America's great competitive advantages.

In an increasingly competitive global marketplace and in the diplomatic corridors of power, America still stands alone.

Our future is in our hands.

But our hands must be strong, nimble, and confident, for history shows that great countries and civilizations often fail due to one or more of three shortcomings: a lack of fiscal discipline; a culture that does not promote risk taking, openness, scientific innovation, or the common good; and a foreign policy not grounded in the national interest and executed at the extremes of isolationism or foreign interventionism.

America has been blessed by geography, ample natural resources, and a free form of government that allows it to be strong, secure, and independent even as it participates fully in the global marketplace.

America is a great and good country but it can be greater and better. Especially now, it needs to recapture its jaunty "why not?" spirit, because America can hardly afford to stand still. It needs a spurt of creativity and growth that resembles the period in the early twentieth century when it first emerged as a major player on the global stage.

Here is how Charles Morris describes this era in the opening of his book *The Tycoons*:

> America was not only the most populous of industrial countries but the richest by any standard: per-capita income, natural resource endowment, industrial production, the value of its farms and factories. It dominated world markets—not just in steel and oil

but in wheat and cotton. It ran huge trade surpluses in goods and was gaining preeminence in financial services. Its people were the most mobile, the most productive, the most inventive, and, on average, the best educated. Attentive European elites were shocked as they came to understand the scale and speed of America's ascendancy.

Senator Chauncey Depew of New York welcomed the new century with these words:

There is not a man here who does not feel 400 percent bigger in 1900 … bigger intellectually, bigger hopefully, bigger patriotically … from the fact that he is a citizen of a country that has become a world power for peace, for civilization, and from the expansion of its industries and the products of its labors.

Or as the historian Gordon Wood described America at its economic surge was just getting under way, "Something momentous was happening in the society and culture that released the aspirations and energies of common people as never before in American history." This "something momentous" was the beginnings of American capitalism and an industrial revolution.

We need to renew these "energies of the common people" on a grander scale. Even though the American economy is now much more than just an industrial power, many of the comments about America in the above passage are still apt today.

America is still home to 700 of the world's largest 2,000 companies and 14 of the largest 30 multinational companies. Coca-Cola sells its products in over 200 countries, and McDonald's has 32,000 restaurants spread all over the world. We also lead in global entrepreneurship and philanthropy. The vitality of the American economy is highlighted by the fact that only twenty of the current Fortune 100 companies were even around in 1980. Despite the current upheaval in financial markets, we still have the deepest and most liquid capital markets in the world.

> I don't know about you, but I want America to remain the world's lead actor.

But it appears that I have more confidence in America's future than most. A recent poll by the Chicago Council on Global Affairs indicated that 55 percent of those polled believe that the United States will be equaled or surpassed as a global power over the next fifty years. The Chinese polled believe that their country will catch up to America in terms of global influence within ten years.

Every four years, the National Intelligence Council—which oversees America's patchwork of intelligence agencies—releases a global trends report, which is given to the new president. The latest report, published in November 2008, noted that "the most dramatic difference" between the new report and the one issued four years ago is that it now foresees "a world in which the United States plays a prominent role in global events, but the United States is seen as one among many global actors."

I don't know about you, but I want America to remain the world's lead actor.

My view is that while the world is clearly filling in, and emerging competitors like India and China are catching up with us quickly due to rapid advancements in technology and communications, the American economy is more than holding its own. But without significant pro-growth reforms and more robust economic growth, our lead will diminish incrementally.

Our debt, and our growing dependency on foreign governments to finance it, presents perhaps our greatest challenge. As Ronald Reagan put it, "It is hard to ride tall in the saddle when you owe everyone in town." To paraphrase the former French President François Mitterrand, "Growth is in the East and debts are in the West."

But while many are intimidated by China's supercharged economic growth rates, Russia's petro-driven foreign exchange reserves, and the growth of Middle Eastern sovereign wealth funds, I see the bigger picture—and would take

America to come out on top in the arena of global competition any day of the week.

Russia's embrace of authoritarianism and cronyism, India's dysfunctional bureaucracy, and the fact that thirty-four of the largest thirty-five companies listed on the Shanghai Stock Exchange are still partially or fully owned by its government are just some indicators of the need to take a closer look before throwing in the towel.

Is it unrealistic to merit this description of America's overwhelming competitive position following World War II by British historian Robert Payne:

> She sits bestride the world like a Colossus; no other power at any time in the world's history has possessed so varied or so great an influence on other nations.... Half of the world's wealth, more than half of the productivity, nearly two thirds of the world's machines are concentrated in American hands; the rest of the world lies in the shadow of American industry.

Perhaps this dominance is elusive and indeed unhealthy, but amid the current financial turmoil and angst about America's future glory, let's all appreciate the tremendous achievements of the past twenty-five years. There is much to be proud of and thankful for.

David Smick sums them up well in his recent book, *The World is Curved*: the creation of 40 million new American jobs, the Dow going from 800 to a high of 12,000, and the net worth of Americans going from $11 trillion to $56 trillion.

They are equally impressive for a world that adopted pro-market economic policies and a free form of government championed by America. In 1975, only 25 percent of the countries in the world were democratic, but by 2000, this had grown to 60 percent. During this period, more than 1 billion people had been pulled out of poverty, while from 1950 to 1980, world poverty actually increased.

This is a record to be proud of, not one to run away from or apologize for.

America's periodic angst about its future tells us more about mood swings than indications of decline. Samuel Huntington identified five phases of what he called American "declinism" in postwar America: 1) after the Soviets launched Sputnik in 1957; 2) after Nixon's announcement of multipolarity in the late 1960s; 3) at the time of the oil embargo in 1973; 4) after Soviet expansionism in the late 1970s; and 5) after the Reagan administration's expanding trade and budget deficits. To these I would add the more recent collapse of the tech bubble and the conflicts in Iraq and Afghanistan.

Unfortunately, a negative view of America's accomplishments has spread, amplified by our media. A healthy degree of self-criticism is one thing, a barrage of self-doubt and cynicism is another. The late Lionel Trilling used the phrase "adversary culture" to describe this attitude and Irving Kristol addressed this problem decades ago:

It is not uncommon that a culture will be critical of the civilization that sustains it—and always critical of the failure of this civilization to realize perfectly the ideals that it claims as inspiration   but to take an adversary posture toward the ideals themselves? That is unprecedented.

Today, it seems there are more commentators on the inevitable decline of America than the doers and leaders that will prove the critics wrong again by leading the country forward. Being a bit anti-American not only is socially acceptable in Europe but rather is a badge of sophistication. This was true even as the United States had higher rates of economic growth, had lower unemployment, and was home to brilliant start-ups like Google. The University of Colorado has produced four Nobel Prize winners during the last twenty years, while Oxford University produced none. During one lunch, four Walt Disney creators came up with the ideas for the blockbusters *A Bug's Life*, *Finding Nemo*, *Monsters Inc.*, and *Wall-e*.

To begin changing the perception that America might be losing its edge, let's take a look at America's relative strengths and weaknesses and see how they stack up against the competition. My goal is twofold: to reassure readers who are likely a bit discouraged about America's current standing in the world and to highlight that the world is filling in and we need at all costs to avoid complacency.

Here are the ten benchmarks:

1) Protects citizens' political, religious, and economic freedoms

2) Provides educational opportunity for all

3) Fosters openness, flexibility, innovation, and mobility

4) Ensures a strong defense and conducts a foreign policy based on the broad national interest

5) Nurtures a culture of risk taking and second chances while accepting inequality of results

6) Ensures an independent judicial system and enforces the law in a fair, transparent, and consistent manner—not based on ethnicity or gender

7) Prizes a tradition of service and philanthropy

8) Conserves and uses natural resources wisely

9) Puts in place a low, fair, and simple tax system

10) Maintains a quality health care system open to all

There is obviously some overlap between a few of these benchmarks, so let us begin with some of the broader themes and go from there.

- ## *Protects Citizens' Political, Religious, and Economic Freedoms*

> *"Democracy is the worst form of government, except for all the others that have been tried."*
>
> —Winston Churchill

This is a big one, the foundation of why America broke from the mother country to become independent and free. Our political system, for all its faults, has endured, and the electorate has been steadily broadened. The United States is the world's oldest constitutional democracy, in place since 1789, and its size, culturally and ethnically diverse population, and republican form of government, which reserves significant powers to the state and local levels, all promote a competitive climate.

The peaceful and orderly transfer of power, one of the greatest concerns of our Founding Fathers, has proved ill founded. Our two-party system has also been a key advantage, especially compared with the coalition-style governments of many European and Asian democracies, where a government can fall unexpectedly if a faction withdraws support. In India's election ending in May 2009, a mind-boggling forty-seven parties participated. Japan has had four prime ministers in less than four years, and in 2008 Thailand had three prime ministers in four months. A relatively small communist faction in India's past governing coalition held it hostage by blocking important economic market reforms.

Some emerging market countries in Asia, such as China, cannot embrace the concept of a loyal opposition. It is alien to their culture but crucial to the functioning of a democracy.

Importantly, the American system goes beyond religious tolerance in refusing to establish a national church and in recognizing that all citizens, as a matter of right, are free to practice their religion, including the opportunity to do so openly, without restriction. This is the difference between "religious freedom" and "freedom of worship."

Alexis de Tocqueville noted in 1835, "America is the place where the Christian religion has kept the greatest real power over men's souls" and "the religious atmosphere of the country was the first thing that struck me on arrival in the United States." The variety of the American religious scene was its distinctive feature. In addition to Judaism, it included among others Presbyterians, Roman Catholics, Congregationalists, Methodists, Baptists, Episcopalians, and Lutherans plus the Quakers, Mormons, Amish, and Shakers.

The importance of Christianity in the American story cannot be overstated. It shaped our culture and character, and it acted as a national conscience in spurring reforms and establishing educational and charitable institutions. Christianity also supports the tenets of capitalism, democracy, and scientific discovery. Indeed, Rodney Stark in *The Victory of Reason* asserts that "the modern world arose only in Christian societies."

While China has certainly embraced capitalism, its leadership continues to be wary of religious freedom and Christianity, even though it realizes its vital role in the success of the West. A leading Chinese scholar cited in David Aikman's *Jesus in Beijing* sums up this sentiment nicely:

One of the things we were asked to look at was

what accounted for the success, in fact, the pre-eminence of the West all over the world. We studied everything we could from the historical, political, economic, and cultural perspective. At first, we thought it was because you had more powerful guns than we had. Then we thought it was because you had the best political system. Next, we focused on your economic system. But in the last twenty years, we have realized that the heart of your culture is your religion. That is why the West is so powerful. The Christian moral foundation of social and cultural life was what made possible the emergence of capitalism and then the successful transition to democratic politics. We don't have any doubt about this.

In our judicial system, a person is considered innocent of a crime until found guilty by a jury of common citizens in a court of law. This presumption of innocence and a fair and speedy trial by jury are the foundation of a democratic society.

In many countries, these rights are not protected in a consistent manner, and citizens do not have confidence in the judicial process due to favoritism and corruption. Interestingly, at the end of 2008, Russia abolished jury trials for terrorism and treason. Britain, the mother country of trials by jury, is seeking to drop them for serious fraud and to ban juries from some inquests. Yet South Korea and Japan are moving in the opposite direction, introducing or extending trial by jury in a bid to increase the impartiality and independence of their legal systems.

Just as vital is the American way of not extending rights to ethnic groups, only to individuals; in this way, all are equal in the eyes of the law, and opportunity is open to everyone who wants to take advantage of it. Respect for the dignity of the individual and life forms the foundation of America. On the curved granite wall cradling Ronald Reagan's tomb is this inscription: "I know in my heart that man is good. That what is right will always eventually triumph. And there is purpose and worth to each and every life."

On the economic rights front, America ranks relatively high but has slipped as a complicated web of regulations and taxes has curtailed its citizens' freedom and flexibility. Starting and running a business is still easier in America than the vast majority of other countries, but there is considerable room for improvement.

The American economy is still the world's largest by a comfortable margin. While services account for more than 70 percent of economic activity, the United States is also the world's largest producer of manufactured goods and the fourth-largest producer of agricultural products.

The annual *Index of Economic Freedom* compiled by the Heritage Foundation and *The Wall Street Journal* measures ten economic freedom benchmarks. Its findings capture America's strengths and weakness well. In its 2009 index, the United States ranks sixth overall, behind Hong Kong, Singapore, Australia, Ireland, and New Zealand and just ahead of Canada. America ranked highest in the areas of business freedom, labor freedom, and property rights, but was weak in fiscal freedom and government size.

Starting a business takes six days in the United States,

compared to the world average of thirty-eight days. Obtaining a business license takes much less than the world average of eighteen procedures and 225 days. Bankruptcy proceedings are very easy and straightforward.

The study found U.S. tax rates relatively burdensome. Both the top income tax rate and the top corporate tax rate are 35 percent. Other taxes include a property tax, an estate tax, and excise taxes, and additional income and sales taxes are assessed at the state and local levels. In the most recent year, overall tax revenue as a percentage of GDP was 28.2 percent. Total government expenditures, including consumption and transfer payments, are high. Government spending has been rising and in the most recent year equaled 36.7 percent of GDP.

On the other hand, property rights are guaranteed, contracts are very secure, and the judiciary is independent and of high quality. A well-developed licensing system protects patents, trademarks, and copyrights, and laws protecting intellectual property rights are strictly enforced. The United States' highly flexible labor regulations enhance overall employment and productivity growth. America is also a leader in fighting corruption and has the strongest record of any OECD Anti-Bribery Convention signatory, with 103 prosecutions, a broad scope of coverage, and severe penalties.

Corruption, transparency, and property rights are major and crippling challenges for many emerging countries, including often-mentioned rivals to America, such as China, India, and Russia. Where do these countries rank in the 2009 Index of Economic Freedom? India comes in at #123, China is ranked #132, and Russia grabs the #146 slot.

There you have it. America has a leading record on the political rights front and a solid but slipping position on the economic front, mainly due to relatively high spending and taxes.

The bad news is that the current administration, while cutting some taxes short term to spur the faltering economy, is expected to raise taxes overall. *The Kiplinger Tax Letter* predicts that in 2010, the old 36 percent and 39.6 percent tax brackets on adjusted gross incomes will be restored. The estate tax will need to be addressed before 2011 or the maximum rate will go to 55 percent, with an exemption falling from $3.5 million to only $1 million. The capital gains tax is also projected to go from 15 percent to 20 percent.

The need for America to put in place a lower, simpler, and fairer tax system should be a top priority and will be further discussed later in the book.

• *Provides Educational Opportunity for All*

America provides educational opportunities equal to or better than any country in the world. Student and school performance as well as the issue of equal opportunity across school districts is another matter indeed.

Is the unsatisfactory performance of so many American students due to opportunity or to other factors? This is the great debate, with tremendous consequences because America will not remain the global leader unless opportunity and performance are joined. Like a high-quality slice of Swiss cheese, there are holes where opportunity and achievement are clearly unacceptable. In the next section of this book, we will address how to improve performance by highlighting the issue of responsibility and competition.

Perhaps the most important factor in America's success has been its well-educated citizens and workforce. Only sixteen years after landing at Plymouth Rock, the Puritans established Harvard. In 1647, the Massachusetts Colony enacted a law that all children must attend school. Rodney Stark in *The Victory of Reason* explains that every township with fifty households was required to begin instruction, and those with more than one hundred households had to set up a school. Even before the Revolution, ten colleges were founded in America, while Great Britain had only two. By 1800, there were twenty more colleges in America, and this growth has continued to this day.

> Perhaps the most important factor in America's success has been its well-educated citizens and workforce.

By some studies, the United States is home to seventeen of the top twenty universities in the world. The role these institutions play in America's economy is hard to overstate. The University of California system alone produced more patents in 2003 than China or India. Even a survey of 500 top universities conducted by Shanghai University listed 159 American universities compared to 31 universities for Japan, 30 for China (including Taiwan and Hong Kong), and 2 universities for India (which, by the way, has an almost 40 percent illiteracy rate for women).

But with overall high school graduation rates at 65 percent in an increasingly complex global economy, we have a lot of work to do. A quarter of a century ago, the report *A Nation at Risk* revealed widespread failure in American schools. "If an unfriendly foreign power had attempted to impose on America the mediocre education performance that exists today," the report warned, "we might well have viewed it as an act of war."

Since then, the role of the federal government in education has unfortunately increased. The federal government now regulates policies, such as testing, instruction, and hiring, once handled by state and local authorities. Meanwhile, spending has increased 69 percent in real terms, though we already spend more money per pupil than any country in the world. Today, the average student in American public schools can expect more than $9,200 to be spent on his or her behalf by taxpayers.

Despite this, one in three fourth-graders scored "below basic" in reading on the National Assessment of Educational Progress. Among low-income students, only half passed the reading test.

State and local authorities are in a better position to improve schools. The most promising education reforms launched since 1983 have occurred at the state level. State-level innovation has been the catalyst for promising education reform ideas like charter schools and teacher merit pay.

We can't allow another twenty-five years to pass without real progress improving elementary and high school public education in America. Freedom comes from knowledge. More on what we can and should do to improve education is around the corner. One basic principle: put parents squarely in the driving seat.

• *An Open Society and Economy*

America's open society and economy is its ace in the hole.

At first glance, you might think that a more independent America would be tantamount to a closed, inward-looking society and economy. This would be a sure prescription for American decline.

Rather, America is perhaps unique in the opportunity to be both fully open to the world and independent. American business is "open for business" worldwide, and one of America's key competitive edges is that it is open to new ideas, people, capital, and products. This is why we are the innovation nation (and need to stay that way). Innovation leads to progress, growth, and prosperity.

Openness also leads to a curiosity about the world and guards against overconfidence and complacency. Barbara Tuchman described the closed British attitude at the time of our Revolution as a "sense of superiority so dense as to be impenetrable." A similar lack of curiosity in the world led to the downfall of the Chinese empire. One example of America's openness is the number of foreign students at our universities and colleges. Last fall, five of the six top-ranking students at Yale University were from overseas: China, Germany, Moldova, Slovenia, and Turkey. America also leads the world as home to 22 percent of those students who chose to study abroad.

We also benefit from being open to legal immigration from all over the world. According to research by Vivek Wadhwa published in *BusinessWeek*, about half of Silicon Valley start-ups were founded by immigrants over the last decade. These immigrant-founded technology companies employed 450,000 workers and had sales of $52 billion in 2006.

His research found similar trends when examining global patent filings by foreign nationals residing in the United States with the World Intellectual Property Organization of Geneva. Foreign nationals residing in the United States were named as inventors in 25.6 percent of international patent applications filed from the United States in 2006, up from 7.6 percent in 1998. When trying to understand the reason for the 337 percent increase, Wadhwa discovered that as of September 2006, there were 1,181,505 educated and skilled professionals waiting to gain legal permanent-resident status. This can take a decade—far too long for creative people longing to become American citizens.

Our average tariff on imports is just 1.6 percent compared with a world average of about 5 percent, with many foreign countries blocking U.S. goods and services with impenetrable nontariff barriers and regulations. America also remains open to foreign investment, provided that it is by private companies in areas outside of national security. Reasserting a longstanding U.S. policy to treat foreign investors the same as home-grown ones, in 2008, President Bush reasserted that America "unequivocally supports international investment in this country."

American society is also more socially fluid and egalitarian than any other, and this is true even for people from vastly different economic situations. Alexis de Tocqueville noticed this egalitarianism more than a century ago, and it remains the norm today.

> In other countries, if you are rich, powerful, or from a certain group or caste, you are surrounded by the trappings of aristocracy, which is the pleasure of being treated as a superior person. In India, for example, the rich enjoy the gratification of subservience, of seeing innumerable servants attend to their every need. In America, however, no amount of money can buy you the same kind of attitude.

America is the only country in the world where a waiter or taxi driver is called "sir," as if he were a lord or knight.

• *Land of Second Chances*

In many countries, one's future is set at the time of birth. Due to ethnicity or economic class, opportunities for advancement are at best limited. In some cases, high levels of academic achievement can lead to social and economic mobility, but even this is at best a slim chance.

The rags-to-riches stories that reflect the openness and mobility of America are endless and inspiring.

At age six, Oprah Winfrey was living with her grandmother in poverty. Nevertheless, Oprah was able to overcome those initial setbacks, and now she is one of the most powerful women in the world and is greatly admired for her empathy and generosity.

Kirk Kerkorian, son of Armenian immigrants, dropped out of eighth grade and took up boxing. The amateur fighter threw punches under the name "Rifle Right Kerkorian" and flew planes across the Atlantic during World War II. He made his first bundle selling Trans International Airlines in the 1960s, investing the proceeds in Las Vegas. Today, his MGM Mirage has more than half the hotel rooms on the Las Vegas strip.

Walt Disney grew up in a poor family under a repressive father, who confiscated his hard-earned paper route money to put food on the table. Fired by a creative imagination and a love of animation, he incrementally built Disney into perhaps the most recognized brand in the world.

Steve Jobs was adopted into a working class family and grew up in apricot orchards that would later become Silicon Valley. Dropping out of Reed College because he couldn't pay the tuition, he cofounded Apple in his parents' garage in 1976. After a 1985 power struggle with John Scully, he left the company to create Pixar, sold it to Disney, and then returned to Apple in 1996 to launch a series of brilliant new devices.

Ralph Lauren, son of Russian immigrants, was born and raised in the Bronx, where he shared a bedroom with two of his brothers. At age twelve, he worked after

America is the only country in the world where a waiter or taxi driver is called "sir," as if he were a lord or knight.

school in department stores to help pay for his fancy taste in clothes. Eventually, he dropped out of City College to launch Polo Fashions with a $50,000 loan.

Some cynics may scoff at these stories as one-in-a-million cases, but they send a powerful message to young Americans and the world: with ambition, hard work, persistence, and creativity, anyone can achieve his or her dreams. There is no such thing as failure in the land of second chances. Americans are nimble at changing careers in midlife, moving West to seek opportunities, and creating ventures to begin anew.

An important part of maintaining this culture of opportunity is to accept that setbacks are part of the process. Some, by dint of background, skills, and yes, luck, will achieve more than others. Accepting an inequality of outcomes is vital to preserving an environment of opportunity. Unfortunately, it seems that recently, America is more bent on taking steps to ensure more equality of outcomes and incomes than in renewing its commitment to an America unbound by envy or distrust.

> Accepting an inequality of outcomes is vital to preserving an environment of opportunity..

Sometimes, those who have further to climb gain the greatest satisfaction from their accomplishments. As Walt Disney was fond of saying, "Doing the impossible is great fun." Booker T. Washington, who knew something about struggling for success, put it this way: "Success is to be measured not so much by the position that one has reached in life as by the obstacles one has overcome."

• *Prizes a Tradition of Service and Philanthropy*

On a global scale, no one can match the generosity and goodwill of America. From individuals to companies to nonprofits, such as religious organizations, the scope and intensity of America's charitable leadership is remarkable.

At home, Americans contribute countless volunteer hours of service with schools, hospitals, sports teams, and other worthy organizations and causes. Americans contribute more than $300 billion annually to charitable organizations, with more than 80 percent of this coming from individuals. Claire Gaudiani, author of *The Greater Good: How Philanthropy Drives the American Economy and Can Save Capitalism,* notes that Americans give twice as much as the next most charitable country.

In philanthropic giving as a percentage of gross domestic product, the United States ranked first at 1.7 percent. Britain was next, giving 0.73 percent, while France, with a 0.14 percent rate, trailed such countries as South Africa, Singapore, Turkey, and Germany.

Despite the great economic gains made by emerging market countries, poverty and preventable disease is still widespread. Since 1980, 1 billion have been pulled from poverty, but 2 billion people in the world still live on less than $2 a day, 24,000 children die each week from malnutrition, and most devastating, one half of the world does not know how to read or write!

These are the two faces of Asia: the gleaming towers and bustling markets and the crushing poverty of rural villages and overcrowded cities. China has sharply reduced child malnutrition, and now just 7 percent of its children under five are underweight. In India, despite robust economic growth, the comparable number is 42 percent. A 2009 World Food Program report noted that India remained home to more than a fourth of the world's hungry, 230 million people in all. Most experts agree that providing adequate nutrition to pregnant women and children under two years old is critical.

The U.S. government's official foreign aid to developing countries is significant, at around $25 billion a year—almost twice that of the next country in line. Still, this figure represents but 12 percent of America's overall contribution, according to the *Index of Global Philanthropy* published by the Hudson Institute.

Religious giving alone is close to $10 billion and will soon be equal to half that of official assistance. Payments that American citizens send back to their families living in developing countries will soon reach $75 billion per year. Finally, private capital flows by American companies top $65 billion.

Much has been done but

the remaining global agenda is daunting. Bill Gates regards as the greatest accomplishment of the past five decades the reduction of deaths among young children by 50 percent, to 10 million a year in 2007. The world's most successful capitalist praised the World Health Organization (WHO), while unveiling an ambitious new global plan to eradicate polio within a few years.

• *Conserves Natural Resources and Provides Recreational Opportunities*

> *Conservation means the greatest good to the greatest number for the longest time.*
>
> —Gifford Pinchot

America's conservation movement has evolved over time to become a leader in world efforts to protect and use natural resources in a responsible manner. With nearly 400 national parks and over 5,000 state parks covering 12 million acres, Americans have ample opportunity to experience the beauty of their country. About 29 percent of America's landmass is owned by the federal government. That's an astounding 653 million acres.

In the early years of America, concern about the environment and conserving and protecting resources was certainly less than satisfactory. The appearance that America's resources were endless was probably the major reason. Still, conservation efforts began with the founding of America. Forest management goes back to 1626 in Plymouth Colony, when there were ordinances restricting the sale of timber.

A Library of Congress report on the evolution of the conservation movement from 1850 to 1920 suggests that as the wilderness frontier closed and industry expanded, many of the following factors propelled progress on conservation issues:

- The transformation of society to the new suburban ideal

- The burgeoning interest in camping, recreation, and character development, especially for boys, and formation of scouting organizations

- The use of nature as an instrument of education, as in the urban parks and playgrounds movement, and the movement for "nature study" in schools

- The development of landscape architecture as a profession

- The use of photography to fix the image and identity of the American West

- The celebration of the American landscape as the source of the nation's moral identity

- The development of scenic tourism by railway and eventually by automobile, and the growing recognition of its economic importance

- The growth of leisure time for the new urban and suburban middle class

- The growth of hiking, mountaineering, angling, and game-hunting as recreational activities

- The rise of the leadership class to exercise decisive leadership in many aspects of the movement to conserve natural resources

- The debate over the use, control, and distribution of the nation's remaining public lands and their resources

- The growing recognition of the disastrous consequences of deforestation, particularly in the eastern United States

- The increasing public anxiety over the perceived waste of the nation's natural endowment

- The growing confidence in science to guide human knowledge and action, and in the power of technology to solve human problems

- The creative influence of scientists and engineers on the development of government policy concerning natural resources

Here are just some examples that highlight the nation's growing interest in conservation during this period:

- In 1849, the Department of the Interior was created. American conservationists soon invented the idea of the national park and developed the national park system. In 1875, the American Forestry Association was founded, and in 1891, the national forest system was launched.

- The Forest Reserve Act allowed the president of the United States to set aside forests for the public domain. Within a decade, Presidents Harrison, Cleveland, and McKinley had transferred approximately 50 million acres into the forest reserve system. The U.S. Forest Service was founded in 1905, and soon state and federal legislation was passed to protect certain classes of wildlife and established a system of national wildlife refuges.

All these actions shaped the early American conservation movement and recovered for their nation the truth that what is human and what is natural are parts of a single whole.

It is ironic that Republicans have allowed themselves to be put on the defensive on the environment, given that the father of the modern conservationist movement was one of their own.

> It is ironic that Republicans have allowed themselves to be put on the defensive on the environment, given that the father of the modern conservationist movement was one of their own.

President Theodore Roosevelt wielded his pen to enact muscular conservation legislation that significantly altered conservation policy and attitudes. The concept of stewardship of the nation's resources firmly took root during his administration.

Theodore Roosevelt was a big-game hunter and big-time preservationist. He believed (and I agree) that responsible hunters are great conservationists, and his record will never be surpassed. He began the National Wildlife Refuge System, which has grown to 350 sites and 150 million acres. He insisted that the Grand Canyon be protected from mining interests and be transformed into a 1,904-square-mile national park. He authorized the first federal irrigation project and five new national parks, quadrupled America's forest reserves, and protected an amazing 230 million acres from any commercial development. That represents 10 percent of America's landmass (and by the way, that's including Alaska).

In 1940, the U.S. Fish & Wildlife Service was founded, and it is important to recognize that most conservationist efforts have been led by and funded by fishermen and hunters. In 1934, President Franklin Roosevelt signed legislation that required all hunters over the age of sixteen to purchase duck stamps. Duck stamps play an important role in habitat conservation, because 98 percent of all funds generated by their sale go directly toward the purchase or lease of wetland habitat for protection in the National Wildlife Refuge System. The duck stamp program brings in over $600 million of revenue per year.

America's conservation movement is a partnership of individuals, grassroots organizations, nongovernmental organizations, educational institutions, and local, state, and federal government agencies.

During the last fifty years, America has taken a global leadership role by enacting far-reaching environmental legislation. And unlike the European Union (EU), which all too often has passed grand legislation but is inconsistent in enforcement, American laws have teeth. During the 1960s and 1970s, federal legislation primarily focused on the health concerns of wastewater treatment. The 1980 Superfund Act was a tax on the petroleum and chemical industries to pay for cleaning up toxic land. The five Clean Air Acts between 1963 and 1990 were costly to industry but strictly enforced. In the 1980s, there was a ban on asbestos and chlorofluorocarbons were banned from aerosols. In December 2007, President Bush signed the Energy Independence and Security Act, which created new rules for energy efficiency in cars and houses.

America's conservation movement is a partnership of individuals, grassroots organizations, nongovernmental organizations, educational institutions, and local, state, and federal government agencies. The U.S. Forest Service has set out three important priorities of the conservation movement: climate change, water issues, and the education of the public.

While there will always be a delicate balance and tension between resource users and those seeking to protect natural resources, the conservation ethic in America will move forward; it is a tradition of which we can be proud. Let's end with one startling fact: 40 percent of America's total land area is under the protection of the government.

• *A Foreign Policy Focused on the Nation's Vital Interests*

America's foreign policy has been largely successful.

While protecting America's vital interests, it has blended

American military and diplomatic strength to deter aggression, protect the nation's vital interests, and promote freedom, free markets, and the dignity of the individual. It has also been a force of good in the world.

America's military strength is unquestioned, with a defense budget equal to the next ten countries combined. The U.S. Navy's battle fleet of 281 ships is larger than the next thirteen navies combined, and eleven of those thirteen countries are allies or partners. This dominance is the best guarantee of our security, for one clear lesson of history is that weakness is provocative and peace is best achieved and maintained through strength. One example is the Korean War, which may have been deterred if the U.S. military budget had not been cut by almost 90 percent from the end of World War II.

America's foreign policy has evolved along with its growth and interests. In its first century, the chief goal was to expand westward, avoid unnecessary entanglements, and achieve regional security and hegemony.

Growing economic might and the achievement of these regional objectives led to the next stage of global involvement, beginning with the Spanish-American War of 1898 and then the late but decisive entry into World War I. Entry into World War II, following Pearl Harbor, began the period where America assumed a global leadership role, and its dominant economic and military position following the war led to a strategy of containing Soviet expansionism and communism.

The United States has, of course, made mistakes and at times has overreached and underestimated the difficulty of achieving goals, no matter how noble or worthwhile. America has demonstrated resolution in war and magnanimity in victory. Twice in the twentieth century, the United States saved the world: first from the Nazi threat, then from Soviet totalitarianism. After destroying Germany and Japan in World War II, America proceeded to rebuild both nations, and today they are close and prosperous allies.

The spread of capitalism and freedom around the world in the post-WWII era is indisputable. For the most part, and especially compared to earlier hegemonic powers, America is an abstaining superpower: It shows no interest in conquering and subjugating the rest of the world.

To summarize, across the ten benchmarks that measure the success of a country, America scores relatively high but will always fall short of perfection. Even Sears, Roebuck, where I sold sporting goods during college, offers consumers three choices: good, better, and best. I like to think that America ranks better or best pretty much across the board.

My hope is that this discussion has renewed your confidence in America's future and has you rubbing your hands together to get into how we can make it even better. Peggy Noonan, in a *New York Times* op-ed, summarized just why we should look ahead with a jaunty attitude brimming with "why not?" confidence:

> This is a good time to remember who we are, or rather just a few small facts of who we are. We are the largest and most technologically powerful economy in the world, the leading industrial power of the world, and the wealthiest nation in the world.

"There's a lot of ruin in a nation," said Adam Smith. There's a lot of ruin in a great economy, too.

We are the oldest continuing democracy in the world, operating, since March 4, 1789, under a vibrant and enduring constitution that was formed by geniuses and is revered, still, coast to coast. We don't make refugees, we admit them. When the rich of the world get sick, they come here to be treated, and when their children come of age, they send them here to our universities. We have a supple political system open to reform, and a wildly diverse culture that has moments of stress but plenty of give.

Part Two

America's Challenges
Abroad and at Home

America has been blessed with many advantages and is currently perched on top of the world. The key question is, will it be able to stay there? No doubt it faces stiff challenges from a rising Asia and a world filling in due to tremendous progress by emerging market economies. These countries have benefited by advancements in technology and communication, not to mention market reforms and access to global markets.

Some believe the future belongs to Europe, emerging market countries such as China and India, or the Asia-Pacific region. But there is perhaps a much greater challenge we need to face—ourselves. Our current financial problems should be a giant wake-up call to all Americans. We need to make some significant changes and confront both internal and external challenges or risk incrementally losing our lead over our competitors. Let's start by assessing some of our competitors and then address how we need to change ourselves.

Europe's Grand Alliance

The European Union, a collection of twenty-seven nation states, is not a superpower, but European multinationals are world-class competitors. In addition, EU rules and regulations can (and do) stymie many American firms eager to penetrate its market of 350 million consumers.

British Foreign Secretary David Milibrand, in a late 2007 speech to the College of Europe, acknowledged the limitations of the European Union:

> There is only one superpower in the world today: the United States. There may be others on the horizon, such as China and India, but the United States has enormous economic, social, cultural, and military strength. In terms of per-capita income alone, it will remain by far the dominant power for my lifetime.

Europe suffered tremendously, both financially and in human terms, from two devastating world wars, with millions dead, wounded, and homeless, and hundreds of cities and towns spread over a dozen nations laid to waste in less than thirty years. Sir Winston Churchill and the father of the European common market Jean Monet both believed that the only way to avert a future calamity was to unite the former warring countries through a common market, common currency, and united interests in peace. They spoke often of a United States of Europe.

Sixty years later, not only has the European Union been created—complete with a capital, a democratically elected parliament, a flag, and an army—but the unthinkable also occurred: they created a common currency on January 1, 2002, the euro, which has become a significant rival to the U.S. dollar in global trade.

Europe also generates an annual gross national product about $1 trillion larger than America and its economic prospects vary region by region. Scandinavian Europe offers fiscal discipline and outward looking multinational companies such as Nokia. Atlantic Europe contains nation states with an imperial history and a lasting diplomatic clout. Central Europe is lead by Germany, a powerhouse exporter and the third largest economy in the world. Eastern European countries are captivating investors with their growth potential and vitality.

Europe has several impediments to challenging America on the global stage. First is demography. Almost all the nations in Europe have shrinking populations and have absorbed just about all the immigration they can culturally and politically handle. This demographic problem exacerbates the reality that it will be increasingly difficult to finance Europe's generous welfare state. It is also interesting to note that its twenty-seven member countries, taken together, cover an area about half that of America.

Next, the EU's growing bureaucracy in Brussels is lampooned by many member countries, which highlights the divisions among the different regions and cultures regarding very basic issues of governance. Rather than unity and harmony,

discord and conflict reign supreme. Perhaps most importantly, the EU has no basis for conducting a foreign policy
and is a paper tiger in terms of the size of its military and its
will to fight. European nations—with almost 2 million men and
women under arms—are only able, at best, to deploy around
fifty thousand at any one time. EU countries have around
1,200 transport helicopters, yet only about 35 are deployed in
Afghanistan.

Emerging Market Competitors

Emerging market countries, formerly referred to as developing
nations, are a major global force whose economic growth and
political and diplomatic impact will be enduring. Emerging market
countries account for 83 percent of the world's population,
produce 25 percent of global GDP, and over the past five
years have collectively generated roughly 50 percent of global
economic growth.

What has fueled this surge? With the tremendous breakthroughs in telecommunications and technology over the past
decade, emerging market companies have exploded onto the
global economic scene, attracting unforeseen levels of foreign capital anxious to tap into its growth potential. Economic
policies in many emerging market countries have become
markedly more open and pro-market.

This shift in global economic wealth and power has become
a commonplace topic of pundits. Almost everyone in the West
now speaks with awe of the pace of China's rise, India's emergence as a geopolitical player, Russia's petro power and the
growing role of regional powerhouses like Brazil in interna-

tional relations. Let's briefly assess the strengths and weaknesses of each of these countries.

• *China Surges*

China is perhaps in the best position near term to increase its influence and power at the expense of the United States. It also faces significant obstacles and a couple of giant speed bumps that could derail its ambitions.

If you lay a map of China over one of the United States, some striking similarities emerge. Both account for almost exactly 6.5 percent of the world's landmass, and their shapes are also broadly similar. China's population is, of course, more than four times that of America's, and this seems to me to represent a weakness rather than a sign of strength. The geographic imbalance in economic wealth, with China's eastern seaboard making enormous strides and the rural, inland areas much less so, has led to tension, strife, and potential political instability. Agriculture accounts for 11 percent of China's GDP but 43 percent of total employment.

From 1842 to 1979, the Chinese experienced foreign occupation, civil wars, the invasion by Japan, and the Cultural Revolution. China's economic growth story began in 1979 and has thus far been underpinned by the following: urbanization, tight control of currency and banking, huge investments in infrastructure, foreign direct investment, and export-led growth. Underpinning this strategy is the energy, drive, and ambition of the Chinese people. They share an unquenchable desire to improve themselves and their country.

Still, the great strides the Chinese economy has made make it easy to forget that China's per-capita output is less than Albania's. In purchasing power parity terms, China ranks one hundredth. The next stage of growth may also be a bit more difficult, since foreign investment and key export markets are declining, while the Chinese consumer is reluctant to take up the slack in a period of economic uncertainty. Chinese households save about 35 percent of their incomes, for many reasons, such as the lack of any government safety net.

A thorough review of the competitive framework between China and America could easily be a book in itself. Let me pause to weigh in on the side of America.

America has a more durable rules-based society relative to China's more fleeting relationship-based culture. America's democratic government is more flexible and adept at fixing problems while China's autocratic government will have more problems changing course. America's openness, transparency and freedom will best China's controlled, opaque and restrictive approach. America's demographic edge of a more youthful country open to immigration will fare better than China's rapidly aging population due to its one child policy. Unlike Japan, China will likely grow old before it grows rich.

America also has a geographic advantage being surrounded by two oceans and friendly allies. China borders countries such as India and Russia that harbor historical and mutual grievances. China's pricing and cost advantages in manufacturing have narrowed considerably while America's economic strengths and productivity are on the rebound. America has the key advantage of having a currency with world reserve status whereas China has a controlled and restricted currency that is substantially undervalued.

I could go on but the bottom line is this: what country do

people around the world want to emigrate to for opportunity and a better way of life? The global investment guru Joe Rogers, who is so negative on the future of America and so bullish about China's future prospects, moved his family to Asia. I found it interesting that instead of relocating to China – he chose Singapore.

These political issues go to the heart of China's chief handicap – central control by an anointed leadership class. Many point to this as a major advantage over its rival India that, as the world's largest democracy, has to deal with all the frustrations of making decisions through the democratic process. I beg to disagree and see the Chinese political model as a major speed bump down the road.

A lack of openness, flexibility and respect for the concept of a loyal opposition handicaps China in dealing with other countries as well as internal dissent. The riots in Tibet last year have been followed by other even more serious instability. President Hu Jintao rushed back from a G-8 meeting recently to confront violent unrest on China's flanks in Xinjiang province. This is serious business.

A series of government policies in the western desert region of Xinjiang, a lightly populated area that covers about a sixth of China's total landmass, has for many years led many of the regions's 10 million Uighurs to believe their cultural and religious freedoms were under attack by the Han Chinese, the dominant ethnic group in China.

Like the persistent divide between the more affluent coastal regions tied to the global economy and the inland rural areas that have always lagged behind, the Chinese leadership seems to view these issues only through economic lenses

If China can manage these contradictions and challenges, it will continue to prosper and rise. It will also likely emerge from this global slowdown in fighting trim. Its leadership has kept a sharp focus squarely on growth and productivity and seems to be making all the right moves. China's $600 billion stimulus package is really aimed at infrastructure and includes ample subsidies for research and development. While U.S. banks struggle, China's banks, under government direction, have increased lending 400 percent. Its state investment funds are scouring the world to scoop up undervalued companies in key industries. Lower inflation and lower wages are increasing its price competitiveness, and shipping costs have plummeted as well. China has also made a major commitment to worker training, with 4 million workers in Guangdong Province alone in vocational training.

• *India's Ambition*

India has four times the population of America but covers a land area one third the size. It represents democracy on a grand scale. India's competitive advantages are its well-educated elite, its technology prowess, its youthful population, and a democratic form of government. India's median age is just twenty-three years, compared to thirty-two years for China.

Unlike China, India is a services-driven economy, with this sector representing 53 percent of GDP and 30 percent of the jobs. In contrast, industry is 29 percent of the economy and just 12 percent of jobs. Like China, India has a significant population of indigent farmers. According to *The CIA World Fact Book*, the agriculture business constitutes just 17.8 percent of GDP, but 60 percent of all jobs. This has significant political ramifications. One is that parties representing rural constituencies are beholden to preserving the status quo and block market reforms at every opportunity.

The Congress party led coalition victory in May 2009 is a positive development but its impact on fostering economic reforms to significantly improve India's economy is questionable. This election was about personality, the extreme positions of the opposition and business as usual.

The continued premiership of Manmohan Singh, 76, is a source of stability and serenity when what India really needs is sustained and substantial reform.

India's competitive advantages are its well-educated elite, its technology prowess, its youthful population, and a democratic form of government.

In fact, while it was common to hear over the last five years that reform was being stymied by the leftist wing of the ruling United Progressive Alliance, it was the Nehru-Gandhi power base led by Sonia Gandhi who opposed many market reforms and bragged about nationalizing the banks. It doesn't seem to me that there is any new mandate for positive change despite a situation that cries out for more competition, private financing of infrastructure such as power, streamlining an obstructionist bureaucracy, fighting corruption, vastly improving primary education and making labor markets more flexible.

Above all, it needs to sharply improve primary education, especially for girls. While each year, India's education system pumps out 300,000 engineers, 15,000 lawyers, and 9,000 PhDs, almost 40 percent of India's women are illiterate, and it has the highest high school dropout rate in the world. A good plan would be to place 100,000 of these newly minted engineers as teachers in primary and high schools.

If it wants to reach a higher economic growth trajectory, India also needs to sharply improve infrastructure. India faces a shortfall of as much as $190 billion shortfall in financing key infrastructure projects, according to a study by McKinsey. About 90 percent of India's roads are unsuitable for loaded trucks, and the ports are already running close to full capacity. The government has identified the need for $500 billion in infrastructure spending between 2007 and 2012 but needs a better plan to attract private financing.

In short, for all its advances, India is performing way below its potential and has a substantially lower growth trajectory than China. Over 40 percent of India's children under five remain malnourished compared to 7 percent in China. China's share of world exports is approaching 10 percent while India's is just 1 percent. China's foreign exchange reserves are six times that of India's and its gross national product and average incomes are almost three times that of India.

• Brazil's Boom

While China and India have received the spotlight as emerging market superstars, keep in mind that Brazil's performance and potential is perhaps even greater. With 190 million people in an area only slightly smaller than the United States, Brazil and its smaller neighbor Chile are changing attitudes toward South America as a whole. But the lingering question is whether Brazil's economic recovery is sustainable, or just the latest chapter in a long book of booms and busts.

Brazil's economic growth has not been in the league of China or even India but has been consistent and impressive. My view is that, so far, Brazil has primarily been an improving balance sheet story, supported somewhat by the commodity boom. Inflation is down from the stratosphere to a manageable 4 percent to 5 percent, it has a trade surplus, and it has about $200 billion in foreign exchange reserves. Its exports and manufacturing base have also markedly improved.

Another key strength is Brazil's energy independence, powered by ample hydroelectric power and huge energy reserves. All of this indicates that Brazil's success is not a mere flash in a pan. Confirmation of this was the upgrading of Brazil's sovereign debt to investment grade status last year.

The worst-case scenario for Brazil would be to bask in this optimism and enjoy the glow from its hard-earned investment grade status. President "Lula" Da Silva needs to tackle some serious issues to build a sustainable platform for economic growth and a continuing bull market. The tax burden needs to drop from its current 50 percent level. Public spending needs to be cut, but also redirected to infrastructure projects. Corruption needs to be sharply curtailed and overregulation slashed, especially in labor markets. Finally, Brazil needs to substantially improve its education standards if it hopes to compete head-on with India and China and bring the third of its population that lives in poverty into the middle class.

• *Russia's Petro State*

Russia is moving in the wrong direction in terms of politics, free markets, and corporate governance. From an economic point of view, it is a pure energy play. Russia's oil, natural gas, metals, and timber account for more than 80 percent of exports and 30 percent of government revenues. This dependence leaves the country vulnerable to swings in world commodity prices. Russia's manufacturing base is in poor shape and must be modernized if the country is to achieve broad-based economic growth. Investment has slowed as crony capitalism has made formerly aggressive investors wary and on edge.

As the West pulls back amid the financial crisis, Russia is looking to Asia to fill the gap. In early 2009, it agreed to supply oil to China for the next twenty years, in exchange for $25 billion in loan guarantees. Russia recently opened its first liquefied natural gas plant to supply fuel to Asia. The plant, built on Sakhalin Island north of Japan and part of the $22 billion Sakhalin 2 development, will greatly expand Russia's natural gas empire.

Two weaknesses for Russia are that its population is shrinking and its oil reserves are on an inexorable decline. Russia's stock market has lost more than $1.5 trillion of value since Dmitry Medvedev took office due to falling commodity prices and heightened perceptions of political risk.

The country has struggled to deal with the volatility of oil prices and the rebound in prices in early 2009 underlines its dependency on the commodity. For every $1 change in the price of a barrel of oil, government revenue goes up or down $1.5 billion.

• *Summing Up and Looking Forward*

America does face significant challenges in the economic arena, from Europe and emerging nations alike, but each of these competitors has its own problems to deal with. It would be a mistake and a grave strategic error to blame our competitors for our current economic difficulties.

Later on, I will present an agenda by which America can actually benefit from the rise of Asia and emerging markets, but first, let's deal with our most important challenge—changing our own country and renewing our prosperity.

Rebalancing America

America is a great and good country, but it can be greater and better. De Tocqueville recognized that "the greatness of America lies not in being more enlightened than any other nation, but rather in her ability to repair her faults." In other words, changing course and turning bright ideas into global leaders.

Let's turn now to restoring more of a balance to eight key relationships that have gotten out of kilter. These imbalances pose a threat to our prosperity and global leadership and are at the root of many of our current economic and social problems. Here they are, in no particular order:

- Risk taking and wealth
- Rights and responsibilities
- Simplicity and complexity

- Diversity and unity

- Dependence and self-reliance

- Saving/equity and spending/debt

- Management and shareholders/boards of directors

- Industry and finance

By "balance," I do not mean a static balance or some position of equilibrium right in the middle. Rather, the goal is some sort of dynamic balance due to pressure from either end of the spectrum.

Let's get started taking a closer look at each of these relationships, how they got out of balance, and the steps we can take to move toward the healthy middle part of each relationship. Above all, we will discuss what economic and political reforms are needed to broaden and deepen our competitive edge to strengthen America's role as first among equals.

Risk Taking and Wealth

"It is impossible to win the great prizes of life without running risks.... Life is a great adventure, and the worst of all fears is to fear living."

—Theodore Roosevelt

The basis of capitalism is weighing potential rewards against risks, making a decision, and then putting capital to work. Taking risks should not be confused with careless speculation or gambling, but rather entails careful calculation and a prudent weighing of the probabilities of success against the sobering possibility of a setback and the proverbial "back to the drawing board."

It is vital to keep in mind that, as the great former CEO of Citigroup Walter Wriston colorfully put it, risk is not a four-letter word. On the contrary, without taking risks, nothing of lasting value can be accomplished. All of America's scientific and commercial achievements were due to individuals taking risks, sometimes despite what appeared to be daunting odds. And economic growth comes only when capital is allowed to flow to its most productive uses—and that means to people and companies taking on these risks.

A culture of risk taking and innovation is at the heart of American capitalism and the process of creating wealth. America's vigor is also closely tied to a culture of second chances. In American society, the only true failure is the failure to try in the first place.

So it is never too late to turn things around. Companies are started by seventy-two-year-old Americans, students go straight from community colleges to Harvard, entrepreneurs go from bankruptcy to net worths of billions, and carpenters become doctors in midcareer changes. IHS Global Insight, a consultancy, calculates that in 2005, companies that were once funded by venture capitalists accounted for nearly 17 percent of America's GDP and 9 percent of private-sector employment.

Wealth should come from talent, risk taking, and innovation.

But recently, the potential rewards of risk taking have become separated from the downside of assuming risk. Rather than tying risk to reward, there has come into place a system that encourages taking a reward and passing on the risk! The direct link between actions and consequences has been weakened and, in some cases, severed. For American entrepreneurs and small business owners, the upside potential and downside risks are stark, but for some executives in large companies and banks, it seems to be "heads, I win and tails, you lose."

The mortgage crisis is a good example of a flawed process, with all the wrong incentives leading to painful results. A mortgage broker is compensated for getting a mortgage approved and executed. The larger the size of the mortgage loan, the larger the compensation to the broker. There are no real incentives for the mortgage broker to dig deeply into the financial situation of the applicant; all the incentives point to doing the bare minimum and getting the business out the door.

> A culture of risk taking and innovation is at the heart of American capitalism.

Now, of course, above the broker is some sort of credit standards and management review, but over time, the standards are relaxed because the initial issuer of the mortgage does not intend to have the loan on its books for very long. The mortgage loan—and the risks that go with it—is soon passed on to another willing party. Perhaps it is Freddie Mac or Fannie Mae, a private investor group, or an investment bank like Bear Stearns.

Here is the big step. Firms like Bear Stearns then sliced and diced the mortgages into portfolios of mortgages and packaged them as securities. These securities were then sold to financial institutions around the world. Even worse, the rating agencies, due to incompetence or conflicts of interest, put their stamp of approval on the credit quality of these baskets of mortgages. The holders of these securities ended up with the risk, while all the other parties in this process took the reward and passed on the risk.

Who stood to gain from this flawed process? People who bought a home with nothing down and nothing to pay for two years; people who had no business pushing such mortgages, but made fortunes doing so; people who had no business bundling those loans into securities and selling them to third parties as if they were AAA bonds, but made fortunes doing so; people who had no business rating those loans as AAA, but made fortunes doing so; and people who had no business buying those bonds and putting them on their balance sheets to earn a little better yield, but made fortunes doing so.

There are plenty of groups to blame for the economic mess we find ourselves in, and Wall Street has taken most of the hits. But Washington is at least, if not more, at the root of what went wrong. The Federal Reserve Bank waited too long to tighten money. The SEC allowed leverage in the banking system to go from twelve to one to thirty to one, meaning there was just one dollar of equity for every thirty dollars of debt. Next in line is Congress. It was essentially co-opted by financial interests and failed miserably in supervising Fannie Mae and Freddie Mac. The patchwork of regulatory agencies were outdated, understaffed, and outgunned by Wall Street innovators who took, as a given, their right to push the envelope.

The credit rating agencies, such as Moody's, Standard & Poor's, and Fitch, have all lost their way, in part because of massive conflicts of interest. Moody's goes back to 1909, and Standard & Poor's and Fitch began in 1924, but the chief problem is that while for much of their history, investors paid for the credit ratings, over time bond issuers became the revenue source for the credit ratings agencies. You don't need to be a lawyer to see the problem with this. In addition, as the financial products being rated became more complex and esoteric, the rating agencies were outgunned and outsmarted by Wall Street. In 2007, 37,000 structured finance products carried the agencies' highest ratings, and 44 percent of Moody's revenue came from rating these complex products, according to Barbara Kiviat of *Time* magazine. The SEC, which has regulatory authority over the rating agencies, needs to make sure that investors, who rely on honest and tough standards, are the ones paying for the rating services.

We also need clear credit policies and tough managers and corporate boards to make sure they are followed. This and more transparency and less complexity will ensure that risks are much better managed.

Just as troubling to me is the emerging dichotomy between those building smaller enterprises and the managers of and investors in huge conglomerates like AIG and Citigroup. For smaller companies, there are no excuses, do-overs, or safety nets. If assumptions are wrong, if the market changes, if mistakes are made, the consequences are painful and perhaps fatal. Then it's back to the drawing board to try again. This dynamism explains why almost 70 percent of America's jobs are created by small businesses.

But for the elite managers of the huge institutions deemed "too big to fail," the federal government is very likely to intervene with generous aid and guarantees at the expense of taxpayers. The bailout of big banks, such as Citigroup, is just one example of this two-track approach, which is unfair and in the end will undermine our overall economy.

In my view, the taxpayers are getting the short end of the stick in these bank bailouts. A fairer solution is for the government to acquire not voting stock but warrants—the option to buy such stock. These warrants would convert to common stock when sold, and a Resolution Trust Corporation-type structure could manage the disposal of these controlling stakes into the hands of private equity investors. New owners would restructure bank operations and put in place new executives.

The initial $350 billion in TARP funding was essentially a "get it out the door" program with no accountability or transparency. I get it that we need a functioning financial system, but banks are here to serve us—we are not here to serve the banks. These mega bailout deals have been far too generous to management and have given short shrift to taxpayers, who are assuming substantial risk with unsatisfactory upside potential. It would have been far better to liquidate Fannie Mae and Freddie Mac by auctioning off their assets instead of giving Treasury a $700 billion credit card.

One has to ponder, are these huge capital injections in our banks like drugs to mask the symptoms, or medicine to cure the disease?

The AIG bonus fiasco was also mishandled by Treasury and Congress. I share the palpable taxpayer outrage at the prospect of paying big bonuses without any clear under-standing of the merits, but the precedents of revoking private contracts and sudden, rash, and poorly thought-out tax legis-lation was equally disturbing. It made America look more like a banana republic than the world's longest enduring democ-racy.

The too-big-to-fail debate will probably never be settled. For AIG, almost all its financial problems come from its Financial Services Division. This group wrote almost $3 trillion in deriv-ative contracts, such as the credit-default swap, which is simply an insurance policy against a bond default. AIG is still on the hook for up to $300 billion in potential losses from these policies, yet AIG's book value is only $50 billion! It is particularly galling that the big bonuses were largely to be paid to employees of this group.

> For smaller companies, there are no excuses, do-overs, or safety nets.

Banks, and primarily the five largest banks, bought a lot of these swaps to hedge against bonds going bad. They were comforted by AIG's credit rating (then AAA), but before long the bonds started to go bad and troubles cascaded for these so-called "toxic assets." The real problem goes back to the Clinton administration, when the Commodity Futures Modernization Act of 2000 was passed. The result was that over-the-counter financial derivatives were free from government regulation from the Commodity Futures Trading Corporation.

Let's now turn to the so-called stimulus package. It would have had a far greater impact on spurring economic growth if it had gotten directly into the hands that create employment, growth, and wealth in America—entrepreneurs. Instead of pumping taxpayer capital into big banks oozing with toxic assets, why not support better run, medium-sized banks or, even better, provide some seed capital to new banks? Taxpayers would likely have garnered nice returns from this forward-looking strategy.

According to a recent article by George Gilder in *The Atlantic,* there are now 741 venture capital firms controlling $257 billion of capital and about 10,000 private equity and hedge funds managing $2 trillion. And don't forget individual investors, pension funds, and other institutional investors. Sure, almost all of these investors have taken a hit during this period of financial turmoil, but you can be sure that they are looking ahead for opportunities. As legendary global investor John Templeton always advised, the best opportunities are always in periods of maximum pessimism.

Entrepreneurs across America are working off this counterintuitive assumption. Two senior biotechnology executives recently left Amgen to launch a new pharmaceutical enterprise. A software manager is raising fresh capital to finance the expansion of a new product. A serial Internet entrepreneur is starting anew, and a venture capital company in Los Angeles is raising money for an eighteen-month-old fund to invest in small private companies. This is just a taste of what is happening underneath the negative headlines.

Even though financing has dried up considerably, Caltech and MIT held a successful enterprise forum on building new ventures in tough times. The Los Angeles Venture Association sponsored an investment forum on "Growing Companies in an Economic Downturn." This attitude of looking for opportunities in a time of financial crisis is what will bring us back to economic growth faster than any government spending.

> The politics of class warfare is a road to nowhere.

How would former Prime Minister Margaret Thatcher come down on the stimulus package as it wound its way through Congress?

Her view is probably close to the sentiments expressed in her autobiography, entitled *Margaret Thatcher: The Downing Street Years*:

As governments tried to stimulate employment by pumping money into the economy, they caused inflation. The inflation led to higher costs. The higher costs meant loss of ability to compete. The few jobs that we had gained were soon lost, and so were a lot more with them. And then, from a higher level of employment and inflation, the process was started all over again, and each time around, both inflation and unemployment rose.

As usual, a dose of logical common sense from the "Iron Lady."

If the goal of the stimulus package was to create jobs, then we need to pay attention to a Chicago-based Grant

Thornton study released to the U.S. Department of Commerce Economic Development Administration. It found that backing business incubators that support entrepreneurs and fledgling, young companies is a more effective strategy in creating jobs. More specifically, incubators create forty-six to sixty-nine local jobs for every $10,000 invested.

The study stressed the fact that business incubators create more jobs at a lower expense to the federal government. According to the research, the federal government spends $144 to $216 per job to create activity in the incubator sector. In comparison, roads and transportation projects generally cost more than $1,200 per job, with 4.4 to 7.8 jobs created for every $10,000 invested.

In his new autobiography, *1,000 Dollars and an Idea*, entrepreneur Sam Wyly praises the privations of failure. As a child, his family fell into poverty when his father's grocery store went bust. The experience "taught me at an early age that failure forces you on to another path," Wyly writes. "You have to go in search of new opportunities." His father found new opportunities: selling insurance and running a newspaper. And Wyly became a billionaire through founding companies like Bonanza Steakhouse, Sterling Software, and Michael's Arts and Crafts.

John Maynard Keynes referred to this entrepreneurial drive as animal spirits. Government needs to encourage rather than impede this engine of economic growth. It is easy to start a new business in America, but then government regulations, taxes, and red tape step in to impede the brave soul who leaves a steady job for a hunch and a dream. There are

27 million small businesses in America that generate almost all new jobs and employ about half of our current workforce.

This would be a perfect time to grow our economy and create better jobs by reducing the tax burden on businesses. A U.S. Treasury report shows that the combined American federal and state business tax rate is the second highest within the OECD. Meanwhile, Germany, the United Kingdom, Ireland, Hungary, Poland, Greece, and South Korea have all cut rates sharply. We should match Ireland's 12.5 percent rate, which ignited its economic boom by drawing in investment from all over the world.

It is job creation in high-value-added, high-income areas that lifts the middle class into a higher standard of living. I understand the importance of a strong upwardly mobile middle class as the anchor of the American economy and political system. Here is what Aristotle wrote in his book *Politics* about the political importance of the middle class to the stability of any society:

Thus, it is manifest that the best political community is formed by citizens of the middle class, and that those states are likely to be well-administered in which the middle class is larger, and stronger, if possible, than both other classes.

The goal should be broad-based economic growth that benefits as many Americans as possible. The politics of class warfare is a road to nowhere. We need more legislators who focus more on baking the economic pie and a lot less on cutting and redistributing the pie.

Above all, we need to applaud, not vilify, those individuals who are able to create great wealth through unusual talent, energy, innovation, and risk taking. The creation of wealth is a good thing for, as the scripture notes, "Sow and ye shall reap for all." But we all should recognize that acquiring great wealth can become a selfish activity, and coveting money for its own sake is wrong. The question is, what does one do with wealth?

Do we invest it in new companies, new technologies, medical research, religious or educational institutions? As former British Prime Minister Margaret Thatcher put it in an address to the General Assembly of the Church of Scotland:

> How could we respond to the many calls for help, or invest in the future, or support the wonderful artists and craftsman whose work also glorifies God, unless we had first worked hard and used our talents to create the necessary wealth?

Rights and Responsibilities

Americans are justifiably proud and protective of their constitutional rights but increasingly lax about their responsibilities. Let's look at a few important areas where Americans need to balance these rights by assuming more responsibility.

• *Responsibility and Free Speech*

Free speech is not an unlimited right. Laws regarding defamation, commercial speech, and obscenity place some limits on this right. The freedom of expression that animates our television shows and movies should also be balanced against the responsibilities to society. Studies show that the average child in America sees 14,000 murders on television by the age of fourteen. When watching sports events and family shows, why should we have to ask our children to cover their eyes and ears for every other television commercial?

• *Responsibility and Health Care*

Each of us has a responsibility to do what we can to keep ourselves as healthy as possible. This is not just a quality-of-life issue but is critical to America's financial solvency. According to data from the World Health Organization and the U.S. Department of Health and Human Services, we spend about $2 trillion, or 16 percent of GDP, each year on health care, and this is projected to increase to 20 percent by 2017. Canada spends 10 percent, Sweden 8.9 percent, and Japan just 7.9 percent. About $1 trillion of annual American health care spending is paid for by entitlement programs like Medicare and Medicaid, so you can see how this could explode our budget as baby boomers age.

On a per-capita basis, annual health care spending in America is $7,026, with Switzerland at $5,878, the United Kingdom at $3,361, and Japan at $2,690. You would think that with all this spending, America would lead the pack in terms of longevity and other measures of well-being, but this is not the case. The United States ranks thirty-fourth in the world in life expectancy at 77.9 years, while Germany and Norway are at 80 years, Italy is at 81 years, Australia is at 82 years, and Japan is at the top at 83.3 years.

A recent Business Roundtable report took a broader approach, factoring costs and benefits into the equation. It compares statistics on life expectancy, death rates, and even cholesterol readings and blood pressures. The health measures are factored together with costs into a 100-point "value" scale. The results are disappointing. The United States is twenty-three points behind five leading economic competitors: Canada, Japan, Germany, the United Kingdom, and France. The cost-benefit disparity is even wider—forty-six points—when the United States is compared with emerging competitors China, Brazil, and India.

The reason for this relatively poor performance is due not only to an inability to control costs but also due to diet, exercise, and lack of attention to preventing serious health issues. America spends about one out of every three health care dollars on hospital care, which is terribly expensive compared to preventive health care, such as routine blood pressure checks.

Yet in a given year, about 50 percent of all Americans do not undertake any routine preventive health care measures. Diet and exercise habits are also going out the window; 40 percent of adult Americans get no exercise at all, and 68 percent are overweight. From 1998 to 2005, adult obesity doubled, and most alarmingly, child obesity rose to 17 percent. Someone born in 2000 has a one in three chance of developing obesity, according to *U.S. News and World Report's* "The State of America's Health in

> From 1998 to 2005, adult obesity doubled, and most alarmingly, child obesity rose to 17 percent.

2009." One in five adults still smoke, and caring for people with chronic medical conditions, many of them preventable, accounts for about 75 percent of national medical spending.

It seems clear that regular exercise and a better diet are the key. Let's just look at the link between obesity and diabetes. According to the Centers for Disease Control and Prevention, Colorado is one of the fittest states in the Union, with an obesity rate of about 15 percent. This translates into a diabetes rate of less than 4 percent. Ten states with obesity rates above 26 percent have diabetes rates of over 10 percent. Whether you are just beginning an exercise program or are an athlete, I encourage you to go to presidentschallenge. org and sign up for a program that suits your personal situation.

One solution may be for more companies to provide financial incentives to encourage preventive health practices. PepsiCo provides employees with such incentives, and it seems to work well. Payments for entering stop-smoking programs and checkups are just a few reasons PepsiCo's health insurance premiums stayed flat while, according to benefits consultant Mercer, average premiums for big companies rose 6 percent.

• Responsibility and Respect

Responsibility is closely tied to the concept of respect, and in particular, respect for institutions and crafts. Columnist David Brooks discusses this, citing the book *On Thinking Institutionally* by the political scientist Hugh Heclo. Brooks writes that rules of a profession or an institution are deeply embedded into the identity of the people who practice them. "A teacher's relationship to the craft of teaching, an athlete's relationship to her sport, a farmer's relation to her land is not an individual choice that can be easily reversed.... The connection is more like a covenant."

These connections to institutions, traditions, and practices need to be renewed. Perhaps part of our current financial troubles is due to a breakdown of this respect and tradition. My first job out of school was with the First National Bank of Boston, the second oldest bank in America. During my first year, I was put through a rigorous credit-training program with an emphasis on credit analysis.

I wonder just how many bankers today go through similar training or worry about the third or fourth backup level of loan repayment. Sure bankers, especially Boston bankers, were a bit stodgy, but I could feel the palpable pride and respect that senior executives felt for their craft and the proud reputation and history of the bank. It pains me to say that the First National Bank of Boston, over time, became part of the Bank of America.

• *Responsibility and Education*

"If a nation expects to be ignorant and free in a state of civilization," Thomas Jefferson warned, "it expects what never was and never will be."

Next, let's turn to the crucial issue of education. As already mentioned, the education of early American workers was perhaps decisive in leading to America's rise as a global industrial giant.

A 2009 McKinsey report, *The Economic Impact of the Achievement Gap in America's Schools,* points out that forty years ago, America was a leader in high school graduation rates. Today, it ranks eighteenth out of twenty-four industrial countries. In 1995, it was tied for first place in college graduation rates. Ten years later, it had slipped to fourteenth. This performance has real economic consequences. The McKinsey team estimates that if the United States had raised its educational performance between 1983 and 1998 to that of countries such as South Korea and Finland, its output last year would have been $1.3 trillion to $2.3 trillion higher—a gain of about 9 percent to 16 percent of gross domestic product.

When I read about how American students lag behind our global competitors in such education surveys, I can't help asking myself two questions: How could young early Americans, with just the Bible and some *McGuffey Readers* in hand, in a small schoolhouse packed with children of all ages, accomplish so much? Why do today's American students, with all the material, technology, and resources at their fingertips, achieve less so?

Perhaps the answer to these questions has something to do with attitude and responsibilities, rather than money and buildings. The right of every child to have the opportunity to gain a great education is also tied to responsibilities.

Parents are the key players in helping their children take advantage of educational opportunity in America. President Reagan aptly stated that "I believe that parents, not government, have the primary responsibility for the education of their children. Our agenda is to restore quality to education by increasing competition and by strengthening parental choice and local control."

Parents need to take more responsibility and need more

say in their children's education. Give parents more ways to choose the school their child attends. Since the 1980s, states and cities have created programs, such as vouchers, education tax credits, and charter schools, that give parents the power to choose their children's school. School-choice programs have been found to improve parents' satisfaction, boost test scores, and foster public-school improvement through transparency and competition.

Of particular concern to all of us is that far too often, there are no parents around to perform this vital mentoring role. The breakdown of the family structure has had a significant negative impact on academic performance. In particular, many boys lack fathers to guide, encourage, and discipline them while serving as good role models.

The responsibility of parents and schools is to retain and reward the best teachers and make sure underperforming teachers find another profession. Malcolm Gladwell cites research that highlights the sizable impact that an especially good teacher has on academic achievement. Erik Hanushek of Stanford University estimates that the students of a very bad teacher will learn, on average, half a year's worth of material in one school year. The students in the class of a very good teacher will learn a year and a half of material.

To find and retain great teachers and guide underperforming teachers in another direction requires a flexible rather than rigid salary structure. Bringing in new teaching talent is best done through apprenticeships, with tough performance standards and resources to make substantial investments in teachers showing natural ability and unnatural enthusiasm.

At ground zero is Washington, D.C., school superintendent

Michelle Rhee. In just one year on the job, she had removed one third of the district's principals, improved test scores, and had the courage to talk openly about the need to replace ineffective teachers. "It's sort of a taboo topic that nobody wants to talk about," she acknowledged in an interview with Nicholas Kristoff.

> D.C. is known as the most dysfunctional and worst-performing school district in the country.... A black child from a low-income family in Washington enters kindergarten at the same level as a comparable child in New York City but is two years behind by the fourth grade.

But where are our budget priorities? In Illinois, an analysis showed that only 45.8 percent of school budgets were devoted to teachers, textbooks, and other basic instructional costs. The rest of the budgets were dedicated to new buildings, liquidating debt, administrative salaries, and a myriad of other expenses that don't touch teachers or children directly. A recent article in *Time* magazine by Amanda Ripley contained a wonderful description of what makes a great teacher:

> Great teachers are in total control. They have clear expectations and rules, and they are consistent with awards and punishments. Most of all, they are in a hurry. They never feel there is enough time in the day. They quiz kids on their multiplication tables while they walk to lunch. And they don't give up on their worst students, even when any normal person would.

While parents and teachers play critical roles, it is an inescapable fact that the prime responsibility for learning rests with the students. They have to be eager to read and learn, be motivated, be disciplined, and strive to do their best. The earlier students capture this attitude, the better, because students who fall behind early are much more likely to drop out of high school. In this competitive global economy, not finishing at least high school is certainly not the path to success. We need to bring high school graduation rates from the present 65 percent to 90 percent. One tough-love idea is to deny a driver's license at age sixteen to young people who are not enrolled and performing satisfactorily in high school. This should get them motivated fast.

> It is an inescapable fact that the prime responsibility for learning rests with the students.

While the quality of America's universities is a major competitive advantage, there is definitely room for improvement. One issue is the gradual but marked watering down of the curriculum. In 1850, Harvard required a course in mathematics or science every semester, and Amherst College was even more demanding. Now even the most prestigious colleges and universities do not require much, if any, science or math courses.

Another challenge is to fight students' false sense of entitlement and the resultant creeping grade inflation—the enemy of distinguished academic achievement and merit.

Professor Marshall Grossman of the University of Maryland expresses the following in an article addressing students' sense of entitlement: "Many students come in with the conviction that they've worked hard and deserve a higher mark.... Some assert that they have never gotten a grade as low as this before."

A recent study by researchers at the University of California, Irvine, found that a third of students surveyed said that they expected a B just for attending lectures, and 40 percent said they deserved a B for completing the required reading. James Hogge, associate dean of the Peabody School of Education at Vanderbilt University, said, "Students often confuse the level of effort with the quality of work. There is a mentality in students that 'if I work hard, I deserve a high grade.'"

Jason Greenwood, a senior kinesiology major at the University of Maryland, echoed that view:

> If you put in all the effort you have and get a C, what is the point? If someone goes to every class and reads every chapter in the book and does everything the teacher asks of them and more, then they should be getting an A like their effort deserves. If your maximum effort can only be average in a teacher's mind, then something is wrong.

Yes, indeed, something is wrong.

Simplicity and Complexity

> *"Making the simple complicated is commonplace; making the complicated simple, awesomely simple—that's creativity."*
>
> —Charles Mingus

It seems that Americans and American businesses are being bound up by ever-increasing regulations, red tape, and a complex tax code.

During the 2008 presidential campaign, amid the global financial crisis, it was par for the course to argue that the cause of our problems was deregulation and that we need to reverse course and increase regulations on commerce and finance.

This diagnosis does not square with the facts, and the prescription would be a disaster for American competitiveness. Certainly, some regulations need to be modernized, the SEC and credit rating agencies do need to do a much better job, but overregulation of our economy by the federal government is already clearly a huge drag on our economic growth and freedom.

According to the Heritage Foundation, money spent by federal regulatory agencies increased 44 percent under the recent Bush administration. The number of pages in *The Code of Federal Regulations* increased more than 4,500 pages, and the cost of new regulations increased more than $28 billion. We hardly need more regulation or federal legislation. In 1950, *The Federal Register* contained 20,000 pages. By 2000, it was 120,000 pages. According to *Chief Executive* magazine, the American economy carries on its back an annual regulatory burden of $1.1 trillion!

• *The Power of the Simple Tax*

> *"Simplicity is the ultimate sophistication."*
>
> —Leonardo da Vinci

Our current tax system is like a clog in our national economic artery, slowing down investment, savings, incomes, and growth. It could also be fatal to America's economic position in the world. While politicians, lobbyists, tax accountants, and lawyers may benefit from our complex tax code, the rest of us lose.

In Washington, many legislators like a complex tax system so that they hand out favors, keep control, and stay in power. Instead of concentrating on increasing the economic pie for all Americans, they take delight in wrangling over how the pie should be sliced.

As Steve Forbes has tenaciously argued for years, a much more simple tax system would go a long way to end the separation of Americans based on class while unleashing America's

> Our current tax system is like a clog in our national economic artery, slowing down investment, savings, incomes, and growth.

economy and energy. I agree with the tax principles laid out by Citizens for Tax Reform: that income should be taxed only one time at one rate and that there should be constitutional protections against future tax hikes.

A simplified tax system would throw out the 9-million-word tax code and replace it with a simple 17 percent tax rate that taxes income only once, rather than two or three times. Tax simplification will go a long way to release the creative genius of the American people and spur economic growth, productivity, savings, and investment.

> More savings means a more independent and secure America.

Due to income exclusions, indexed for inflation, of $12,000 per adult and $6,000 per child or dependent, plus the retention of the mortgage interest deduction, the average family of four would not pay any taxes until their income reached $45,000 (roughly the 2006 median family income), and furthermore any interest on savings or dividend income would not be taxed at all.

There would be no tax on capital gains, no tax on Social Security benefits, no death taxes, and no alternative minimum tax. Businesses would pay the same single corporate tax rate but be able to deduct all business expenses, including capital equipment in the year it was purchased, to expand production in America.

A simple tax means more jobs, savings, investment, and economic growth.

America is the world's largest and most entrepreneurial economy but it is increasingly losing ground to tough foreign competition. This has led to weak growth in personal income, a large and persistent annual trade deficit, and huge budget deficits that are being financed by heavy borrowing from Japan's and China's central banks. In addition, America's savings rate is negative, and its tax rates are high relative to most industrialized countries and significantly higher than its dynamic foreign competitors.

America's complex and outdated tax code is at the core of these problems. There have been 15,000 changes to the tax code since the Tax Reform Act of 1986. U.S. households spend roughly 1 percent of GDP in complying with the income tax system. The U.S. Treasury Department estimates that, on average, the total tax burden on new corporate investment is 24 percent.

A single tax rate is not a new idea. Thirteen countries have this one-rate system. Poland's rate is set at 18 percent, Russia at 13 percent, and Hong Kong at 16 percent. To our north, in 2000, the Canadian province of Alberta created Canada's only single-rate personal income tax rate: 10 percent.

You may be surprised that the Commonwealth of Massachusetts has, for some time, had a single 5.3 percent state income tax rate. There also needs to be a high legislative hurdle to raise this rate. A two-thirds majority in the House and the Senate would be reasonable. In Colorado, the TABOR legislation enacted in 1992 forces any tax increase to be approved by popular vote.

America needs to get ahead of the curve with reform that simplifies the tax code, restrains congressional spending, and encourages savings and investment leading to growth in real incomes due to more high-quality jobs. A simple tax would also increase the savings rate in America.

The U.S. savings rate—the percentage of after-tax income that Americans save—has declined to worrisome levels. In 1984, it was 11 percent, and in 2005, it dropped into negative territory, meaning that Americans were spending more than they earned. In 2009, the savings rate moved into positive territory but this uptick seems to be driven by fear rather than by growth.

While Congress has passed tax incentives to encourage more saving, it has clearly not been enough. About 30 percent of American households have no financial assets, and an additional 20 percent have insignificant holdings. In addition, households who have $2,000 or more in savings are ineligible for many welfare programs, providing the poor with a disincentive to save. Furthermore, 40 percent of Americans don't have any tax liabilities and therefore do not respond to tax incentives.

More savings means a more independent and secure America.

It is important to highlight that the lack of a deep savings pool in America forces it to rely on overseas capital to finance its huge and growing budget deficits. This reduces our negotiating leverage and economic independence.

Diversity and Unity

"The name of American, which belongs to you, in

your national capacity, must always exalt the just
pride of Patriotism."

—George Washington

From our beginnings, the diversity of American citizens has enriched our country, but unity is essential to preserve it.

Our Founding Fathers understood that unlike European countries, with centuries of ethnic continuity, America was founded on a series of ideas shared by citizens who bravely emigrated from Europe to begin a new life. The shared belief in these ideals—expressed so well in founding documents such as our Declaration of Independence and the Constitution—are the basis of our shared culture, history, and language.

Thus we become "from many, one"—e pluribus unum.

Put another way, Americans are not joined by race, religion, or ethnicity but rather by our shared faith in ideals, such as democracy, freedom, equal rights, rule of law, and self-government, as well as by our national pride. Andrew Jackson, our seventh president, who carried a bullet in his chest for most of his adult life, described America as "one great family." A delegate from South Carolina to the colonial congress in New York remarked, "There ought to be no more New England men, no New Yorkers, but all of us Americans!"

The American system went beyond toleration in refusing to establish a national church and in recognizing that all citizens, as a matter of right, were free to practice their religion. This is markedly different from freedom of worship, where all religions are not deemed equal and citizens cannot convert to another without fear of retribution.

We do not extend rights to ethnic groups, only to individuals; in this way, all are equal in the eyes of the law, opportunity is open to everyone who can take advantage of it, and everybody who embraces the law and the American way of life can "become "American."

President Franklin Roosevelt put it well when he stated:

> Americanism is a matter of the mind and heart; Americanism is not, and never was, a matter of race and ancestry. A good American is one who is loyal to this country and to our creed of liberty and democracy.

Our society and our youth are bombarded by the mass media with what separates us into ethnic and racial groups rather than what we have in common as Americans.

But we are now in danger of losing the ties that have bound us together. America is at risk of becoming "out of one, many," as different ethnic groups look inward, rather than outward to American ideals, in forming the foundation of their self-identity. The Bradley Project on America's National Identity recently retained Harris to conduct a study on America's changing identity. Of the Americans polled who believed that there is an American identity, 63 percent thought that this identity is growing weaker and a disturbing 24 percent believed that we are already so divided that a common identity is impossible.

How have we become so divided along ethnic and cultural lines, and how do we get back on track to building a unified country?

First, we need to do a better job of teaching our children about the founding ideals of America—our history, traditions, and beliefs—in a vivid and interesting manner. The teaching of "civics," as it was called in the old days, is in dire need of renewal. The majority of eighth-graders cannot even explain the purpose of the Declaration of Independence. Only a handful of colleges require a course in American history. In short, we are losing our collective memories.

At the same time, our society and our youth are bombarded by the mass media with what separates us into ethnic and racial groups rather than what we have in common as Americans. Our shared history is what we have in common. It is through history that we develop a sense of shared identity and purpose.

Historian Gordon Wood captures this sentiment by writing, "A people like us, made up of every conceivable race, ethnicity, religion in the world, can never be a nation in the usual sense of the word. It's our history, our heritage, that makes us a single people."

Yet in America today, we seem to divide ourselves in so many ways. During the last election cycle, the talking heads consistently broke down the voting and political strategies along racial and ethnic lines. Schools and especially colleges sponsor separate orientation and campus activities for various groups as well as stress ethnic studies over an American history curriculum grounded in our founding documents.

In addition, all sorts of organizations, including our federal and state governments, collect personal data organized by ethnicity and race. My wife, who grew up in the Philippines, became an American citizen six years ago. Recently, my son Robert asked me what ethnic grouping he should check when registering for his school's standardized tests. I told him to make and check a new box titled "American."

Now the U.S. Census has a legitimate purpose, to determine how many people live where in order to help determine congressional districts. The first census was taken in 1790 and asked just a few common sense questions. What was the name of the household, how many males and females lived there, and how many were over the age of sixteen? Compare this with the incredible number of questions pertaining to just race and origin in the current census that has to be completed by law. I just received a census form related to self-employed owners. Regarding the origin and race of owner(s), this survey was not content with broad categories but asked specifically whether one was, Mexican, Mexican American, Chicano, Puerto Rican, Cuban, if American Indian or Alaska Native, what tribe, Asian Indian, Chinese, Filipino, Japanese, Korean, Vietnamese, Native Hawaiian, Guamanian, Chamorro, Samoan, Fijian, Tongan, Argentinean, Colombian, Dominican and, well, you get the picture.

In this shrinking world and global economy, with vast improvements in communications and technology, and greater ethnic diversity, there is also the risk of many to identify themselves as "citizens of the world" rather than American.

However noble this may sound, it is not consistent with reality. A recent promotion for New York University began, "As a global citizen, to whom do I pledge allegiance?" This is a selling point to prospective students and their parents?

There are also many large American multinationals that seem to run from the "American" label, preferring the more nebulous description as a "global" institution. Doing business all over the world is welcome, but let's not try to minimize our home country. It should be a point of pride to be an American citizen or corporation, not something to hide under a bushel basket.

Again, Alexander Hamilton, born and raised in the Caribbean, gets right to the point, as cited in Ron Chernow's masterly biography:

> A dispassionate and virtuous citizen … will scorn to stand on any but purely American ground.… To speak figuratively, he will regard his own country as a wife to whom he is bound to be exclusively faithful and affectionate. And he will watch with jealous attention every propensity of his heart to wander towards a foreign country, which he will regard as a mistress that may pervert his fidelity and mar his happiness.

While prizing our diversity, let's begin shining a spotlight on what unites us as Americans; as Benjamin Franklin said, "We must, indeed, all hang together, or most assuredly we shall all hang separately."

We must also end the practice of dual citizenship. Citizens must choose—do they want to be an American citizen? *The*

New York Times recently did a profile on the increasing trend of dual citizenship.

> A citizen of the United States and New Zealand, she (confidential) travels frequently throughout Southeast Asia. "For obvious safety reasons, I always try and travel and put my visas on my New Zealand passport," she said via e-mail. "On a plane, I don't want to be identified as an American if I have that choice, depending on where I am heading."

Alex Thomas, the corporate manager of Travel Document Systems, a visa and passport services company in Washington, said that some of his clients are "uneasy traveling with a U.S. passport, and if they have an additional passport, they prefer to use it."

To restore a better balance between America's diversity and unity, I suggest the following reforms:

- Stress English immersion over bilingual education.

- Make English our national language.

- End bilingual ballots and dual citizenship.

- Require an American history course at college level with a rigorous grounding in our founding documents. This course would need to be successfully completed before a student could enroll in any ethnic-centered history courses.

- Restore the separate celebrations of Washington's and Lincoln's birthday in place of the current Presidents' Day.

- The federal government should cease collecting personal data on the basis of race or ethnicity.

Dependence and Self-Reliance

"It is hard to ride tall in the saddle when you owe everyone in town."

—Ronald Reagan

In the classic, *The Conscience of a Conservative,* Barry Goldwater sums up the intimate relationship between economic and political freedom:

The Conservative has learned that the economic and spiritual aspects of man's nature are inextricably entwined. He cannot be economically free ... if he is enslaved politically; conversely, man's political freedom is illusory if he is dependent for his economic needs on the State.

Jay Winik in *The Great Upheaval* describes the Americans who greeted George Washington on his triumphant march to assume the presidency in New York as "newly proud, educated, civic-minded citizens; even workmen and artisans were literate and independent."

The troika that underpins the American economic system has been private enterprise, self-reliance, and belief in the magic of the marketplace. The growing involvement of government in our lives, and our dependency on it, saps our energy and creativity. If we continue to slide incrementally into European-style socialism, our days of leadership are limited. "When life becomes an extended picnic, with nothing of importance to do," writes Charles Murray, author of *In Your Hands,* "ideas of greatness become an irritant."

• *Health Care Is the Tipping Point*

We are now at or close to a tipping point in our reliance on government, and the issue that will push us over the edge is nationalization of the health care sector. This is no small matter, since it represents 16 percent of GDP.

A dependence on the state for health care not only is the most expensive and least efficient alternative, it will surely sap the country of its initiative, innovation, and risk taking. A state-managed health care system would also represent a tipping point in America's dependence on the state, since the sector is projected to represent 20 percent of the economy by 2017.

While I am no expert on health care reform, it seems to me that any reforms should adhere to four principles: pooling risks and ownership, choices, markets and competition, and preserving direct patient-doctor relationships. Newt Gingrich writes that even Canada's government-run health care system made it illegal to purchase any health care service also offered by the government,

> A state-managed health care system would also represent a tipping point in America's dependence on the state.

until its Supreme Court ruled that "access to a waiting list is not access to health care."

A competitive public and private system will spur innovation and encourage choice. This option is far superior to a situation whereby the wealthy access a private system and everyone else is forced to use the lower-quality government-run system.

• *Energy Independence*

If Brazil can become energy self-sufficient and independent, so can America. In fact, let's go one step further and become a net energy exporter.

By promoting renewable energy, conservation, and clean coal technologies, and by expanding nuclear power, we can achieve this goal within a decade.

There are two steps to make America a net energy exporter by 2019: Electrify the grid, and shift the mix of fuels we use to generate base load electricity. Right now, it is about 6 percent hydroelectric power, 52 percent coal, 20 percent natural gas, and 22 percent nuclear. We need to get to 5 percent hydro, 25 percent coal, 20 percent natural gas, 10 percent solar and wind, and about 40 percent nuclear.

America needs to take an active leadership role in developing massive amounts of nuclear energy for its own use, as well as for export. Paul Johnson points out that America's aircraft carriers and submarines are almost entirely powered by nuclear reactors, with sterling safety records.

We have the technical expertise and the financing capability to build large-scale, safe, and secure nuclear generators that could be located in protected, remote areas. In

December 1951, America developed the first nuclear reactor in Idaho, which generated enough electricity to light four 200-watt bulbs. There are now 438 commercial nuclear reactors in the world that provide 16 percent of global electricity. In the United States, we have 108 reactors that provide 22 percent of our electricity needs; 73 percent of America's clean energy now comes from nuclear power.

Since 1979, until very recently, no American utility has applied for a new nuclear power plant construction permit. Meanwhile, 80 percent of France's power comes from nuclear power plants, and India and China have nuclear power at the center of their energy plans. India plans on adding eight nuclear plants from 2005 to 2010, and China, which now relies on coal for 70 percent of its energy needs, plans to build forty nuclear reactors from 2005 to 2020. Britain has decided to build a large number of new power plants, and Finland and Sweden are following suit.

I encourage even the most ardent anti-nuclear activists to open their minds to nuclear energy as America's cleanest and greenest energy option. Pick up and read *Power to Change the World: The Truth About Nuclear Energy* by Gwyneth Cravens, and

> I encourage even the most ardent anti-nuclear activists to open their minds to nuclear energy as America's cleanest and greenest energy option.

I am sure your attitude will change dramatically. She points out that nuclear power is by far the best option in generating America's base-load electricity. I am for expanding wind and solar power, but consider these facts: To generate the same amount of electricity from a nuclear plant, situated on just one third of a square mile, you would need a wind farm covering 200 square miles with hundreds of wind turbines over 450 feet high anchored in massive concrete bases. This wind farm would require up to ten times the amount of steel and concrete. Which option do you think is better? Making solar panels using polysilicon is also a dirty job, which is why most panel manufacturing is done in China.

> Electrifying the grid has to be the foundation of our energy policy.

Spent uranium fuel can be recycled safely, as is now done in France, and plans to use thorium as a fuel to generate nuclear energy will lessen this problem, since it burns much more efficiently than uranium. It is also safer since the by-product of a thorium-fueled reaction creates plutonium that is unsuitable for use in making nuclear weapons. Thorium is also plentiful. America and Canada each have more than 100,000 tons of reserves, while Australia and India each have 300,000 tons, according to the U.S. Geological Survey. The transition to thorium would also be smooth, since it can be used in existing reactors without major changes.

America would benefit greatly from taking a global leadership role in generating nuclear power: lower costs, cleaner air, export revenues, and of course less dependency on Middle Eastern oil. Keep in mind that 50 percent of the world's natural gas reserves are in Russia and Iran. America can and must become energy independent.

Electrifying the grid has to be the foundation of our energy policy.

Shai Agassi, born in Israel and founder of Better Place, is already working to make this a reality and expand his business globally, as he pursues his vision of building networks of battery-exchange stations in North America, Europe, Japan, and Australia to increase the driving range of electric cars.

Better Place is just beginning to build its first prototype battery-changing stations in countries like Israel, Denmark, and Japan. It hopes to be a critical link in the evolution of the electric-car market.

"The battery is a consumable part of the car, just like gasoline," Agassi said. "Cars in the 1950s only went about 100 miles on a tank of gas, and that problem was solved by installing an infrastructure of gas stations."

Agassi is a vivid example of the "why not?" spirit, starting with the question, "How do you run a country without oil? To get there, you need the number of electric cars coming into the market to exceed the number of gasoline vehicles." Auto companies are now cooperating by spending billions of dollars on electric-car projects, with several models rolling out by 2011. Better Place has teamed with governments in several countries to test its switching stations and has also signed agreements in Hawaii and with a nine-city alliance of communities in the San Francisco Bay Area.

In closing, less dependence on government and foreign

oil would be a welcome change. Next, we tackle an even bigger challenge: reducing our dependence on debt and foreign capital.

Saving/Equity and Spending/Debt

"I am for a government rigorously frugal and simple."

—Thomas Jefferson

Deficit spending financed by foreign capital has become a chronic addiction for America.

This should get your attention. Before you know it, the total interest payments we pay each year ($451 billion in 2008) on our outstanding national debt will be larger than the defense budget. Just as troubling is our growing dependence on financing this debt overseas. Around 1600, the Spanish empire began to crumble when two thirds of its government revenue was needed just to service its national debt.

• Our Chronic Addiction to Debt Financed by Foreign Capital

Close to 30% of our national debt is held by foreign lenders, namely China, Japan, the United Kingdom, and Middle Eastern wealth funds. This trend is escalating, with 75 percent of new debt being purchased by foreign investors. It is fortunate that these pools of international capital are available but unhealthy to depend so heavily on them. Some of these governments do not share our vital interests and goals and, in fact, oppose them. Given America's lack of any savings pool, if these foreign lenders pulled back, even marginally, interest rates for long-term Treasury bonds could jump. We also are sending to China about $50 billion a year in interest payments and the Congressional Budget Office projects that by 2030, we may

Close to 30% of our national debt is held by foreign lenders.

be annually transferring up to 7% of our gross national product to foreign investors as we service our outstanding debt.

Dependence on a rival to finance foreign intervention has a precedent. Historian Niall Ferguson refers to the need of Great Britian to turn to America to finance the Boer War as "an early sign of that shift in the centre of financial gravity across the Atlantic."

Since China has up to 80 percent of its $2 trillion of reserves in U.S.-backed bonds, Chinese leaders have some leverage and have taken on a lecturing tone, referring to these bonds as "China's assets." In March of 2009, Premier Wen Jiabao stated:

Of course we are concerned about the safety of our assets. To be honest, I'm a little bit worried.... I would like to call on the United States to honor its words, stay a credible nation, and ensure the safety of Chinese assets.

That China has gained significant leverage over U.S. policy is a cause for concern. According to *The Washington Post*, about 20 percent of China's foreign currency reserves were tied up in Fannie and Freddie debt last fall, when the two mortgage firms were placed under government conservatorship. Was this decision in part due to pressure from the Chinese government?

China has a number of options to use its leverage to get the United States to do what it wants. The most likely strategy is to threaten to stop purchasing American Treasury bonds or sell its existing bonds. The second is to quietly and systematically reduce its exposure to our government securities. The third option is to publicly dump U.S. debt. This last action would devastate global markets but also significantly damage the value of China's reserves.

On the spending side, there seems to be no sense of restraint whatsoever.

The most likely scenario is a mixture of the first two strategies, while applying pressure on America on a wide range of political and economic issues. "I think what they're trying to say right now is, 'Don't take any steps that would impair our ability to access your market,'" said Auggie Tantillo, executive director of the American Manufacturing Trade Action Coalition, an organization of U.S. businesses critical of China's trade policies. "The Chinese are starting to flex their muscles, they are becoming more powerful commercially and economically, and they want us to know it."

This may be true but America has an even stronger card to play: China is very dependent on the American consumer market, and this fact, if we handle it properly, should more than offset our dependence on Chinese capital.

On the spending side, there seems to be no sense of restraint whatsoever.

Our national debt has gone from $1 trillion in 1980, to $3 trillion in 1999, to $5.7 trillion in 2000, to $10.2 trillion in 2007, and will likely reach $12 trillion by the end of 2009. The U.S. Congress is clearly a spending machine. Former Senate Finance Chairman Bob Packwood recently explained that fifty years ago all governments in the United States — federal, state and local — together spent about 20% of the gross domestic product (GDP). In 2010 it will likely rise to 35% while in Britain it is 40%, France and Italy 50% and in Nordic countries even higher.

Perhaps a better way to evaluate our indebtedness is as a percentage of America's GDP. This has gone from 122 percent right after World War II to 31 percent in 1981; since then, it has climbed back to over 80 percent of GDP.

Then there are state finances. Despite being constitutionally required to balance their annual budgets, many states are deep in the red and are looking to the federal government for help. California is struggling with a $50 billion shortfall, as its cost structure has ballooned along with European-style public sector regulations. Cost for schools, state employees, and health care all grew exponentially in boom times. Government workers enjoy sixteen official holidays, everyone else six. The state dabbled with universal health care and put in place draconian environmental standards. During the last decade, California spending went from less than $50 billion to more than $100 billion.

It gets a lot worse when we add in private debt. The ratio of U.S. public and private debt to gross domestic product reached 358 percent in the third quarter of 2008. This was by far the highest in history. The previous peak of 300 percent was reached in 1933, during the Great Depression.

Nearly all of this debt is private. That reached an all-time high of 294 percent of GDP in 2007, a rise of 105 percentage points over the previous decade. The same thing happened to the United Kingdom, on a yet more impressive scale. This has been a gigantic debt and credit expansion.

Particularly remarkable is the composition of the increased debt. During the 1930s, most private debt was held by non-financial companies. Recently, however, the big increase in debt was in the financial and household sectors. Meanwhile, household debt as a percentage of GDP has gone from 50 percent in 1980 to over 100 percent in 2007, and the total debt of our financial sector has gone from 27 percent to 116 percent of GDP during that same time period.

The savings rate for Americans has gone from around 15 percent in the 1960s to 4 percent in the early 1980s to a negative rate of saving. The average American has nine credit cards with a balance owed of $17,000. The savings rate has marginally climbed into positive territory in 2009 as the great unwinding begins.

While most nonfinancial companies are in pretty good shape compared to banks, the number of triple A-rated companies is dwindling. In 1980, sixty nonfinancial companies held the prized AAA rating. Now just five companies enjoy this coveted status since General Electric fell off the list in 2009.

Then there is the lurking iceberg of entitlement obligations. Social Security, Medicaid, and Medicare will cause federal spending to jump by half, from 20 percent of the economy to 30 percent, by 2035. This tsunami of spending is a major threat to limited government because it runs on autopilot, with automatic increases locked in by each program's governing laws. While other programs are constrained through annual budgets, entitlements get first call on resources. Other goals, such as defense or national security, must compete for an increasingly smaller share of what's left. This "locked-in" spending is steadily undermining the economic future of younger generations.

The Peterson Foundation estimates that in addition to our national debt, we face $6.6 trillion of Social Security and an incredible $36.3 trillion of Medicare unfunded obligations for a grand total of over $56 trillion. This represents $184,000 for every American.

Grover Norquist notes the Bush administration's reflexive "throw money at it" response to every crisis. The response to Hurricane Katrina was $85 billion in public spending. The collapse of AIG, the insurance giant, initially cost $85 billion; Freddie Mac and Fannie Mae, a further $42 billion; and the opening bid of $700 billion for the financial bailout of Wall Street was followed by the $780 billion stimulus package. If we have a problem, we simply throw money at it and hope that it will just go away.

To put these staggering numbers in perspective, the New Deal, for instance, would cost about $500 billion in today's dollars. The Marshall Plan cost a paltry $115.3 billion. The Louisiana Purchase was the deal of the century, at about $217 billion. If you take those three items, add in the adjusted costs of the race to the moon, the savings and loan crisis, the Korean War, the Iraq War, the Vietnam War, and assistance for NASA, you still get to just $3.92 trillion: not even 40 percent of the taxpayers' exposure today.

Under President George W. Bush, federal spending rose from $1.8 trillion in 2000 to just short of $3 trillion for 2008; from 18.4 percent of gross domestic product to 20.8 percent. The new administration's first budget proposal reached $3.7 trillion.

Defense spending has increased in response to Iraq and Afghanistan, but defense spending as a percentage of GDP has been trending ever so slightly lower since the mid-1940s, when it peaked at 37 percent of the total GDP in those war years. From there, each peak since has been progressively lower. During the Korean War, defense spending as a percentage of GDP rose just above 14 percent, having fallen from the World War II peak noted above to approximately 4 percent in the late 1940s.

From the Korean War peak, the number fell continuously, topping out again in the late 1960s during the height of the Vietnam War, just under 10 percent; it topped out again at yet another lower high in the mid-late 1980s at approximately 6 percent. It is now approximately 5 percent, having fallen to a new post-WWII low in 2001, near 3 percent.

Even more disturbing is that Congress has voted away the power of the purse. Now, the lobbyists will appeal directly to the White House, the Treasury, the Fed, the FDIC, and any other applicable bureaucracy for funds during these troubled times. And these unelected officials have no reason not to cooperate.

Congress even seems reluctant to end what appears to be one of the most obvious places to start reining in outrageous spending: earmarks. In early March of 2009, the U.S. Senate defeated an amendment offered by Senator McCain that would have eliminated 9,000 earmarks worth $7.7 billion from the $410 billion spending bill, including the following:

- $2.1 million for the Center for Grape Genetics in New York
- $1.7 million for a honeybee factory in Weslaco, Texas
- $1.7 million for pig odor research in Iowa
- $1 million for cricket control in Utah
- $819,000 for catfish genetics research in Alabama
- $650,000 for beaver management in North Carolina and Mississippi
- $951,500 for Sustainable Las Vegas
- $2 million for the promotion of astronomy in Hawaii
- $167,000 for the Autry National Center for the American West in Los Angeles
- $238,000 for the Polynesian Voyaging Society in Hawaii
- $200,000 for a tattoo removal violence outreach program, to help gang members or others shed visible signs of their past
- $209,000 to improve blueberry production and efficiency in Georgia

Looking ahead, the Congressional Budget Office (CBO) projects almost $10 trillion in additional debt from 2010 through 2019. The administration's 2009 plan is to borrow 50% of every dollar spent. While the CBO projects that nominal GDP will grow by about 50% over the next ten years, it also projects that revenues will grow 100%, which suggests massive future tax increases in relation to GDP are in the cards. The average estimated annual deficit is almost $1 trillion for the next ten years. This is a disaster scenario for America and the U.S. dollar. You can see all the details at www.cbo.gov.

• *Credit Cards Out of Control*

Turning to consumers, credit has been a wonderful option and helped fuel America's consumer economy, but the credit card industry needs serious reform and much more transparency. For every story of a start-up like Google getting off the ground by its two founders maxing out on their credit cards, there are millions of heart-breaking stories of consumers crushed by the weight of credit card debt.

The marketing of credit cards to college students, teaser rates, privacy issues and identity theft, a dispute process tilted against the consumer, pages of fine print the consumer cannot understand, and nonstop marketing and mailing of cards have all led to an explosion of credit card debt and millions of American families mired in debt. There are few lobbies in Washington more powerful than the credit card and banking industry. The industry's most profitable customers, the ones being sought by creative marketing tactics, are the "revolvers": the estimated 115 million Americans who carry monthly credit card debt.

The actual cost of credit card financing is often far greater than expected. Penalty fees and rates are sometimes triggered by just a single lapse: a payment that arrives a couple of days (or even hours) late, a charge that exceeds the credit line by a few dollars, or a loan from another creditor that renders the cardholder "overextended," as defined by the nation's three all-powerful credit bureaus. Just as frustrating for consumers is that just as the Fed cut the federal funds rate down to zero, credit card rates have jumped higher. Bankrate.com reported in March 2009 that the interest rates offered at the ten biggest credit card issuers have doubled or tripled in 2009 and that these hikes are happening even to customers with sterling credit scores. Issuers may be trying to get the most money they can out of consumers before new Fed rules go into place in July 2010 that prohibit them from raising interest rates on existing balances unless the cardholder is more than thirty days late with a payment.

The first logical step at reform is to make sure credit card companies offer full disclosure, transparency, and much simpler agreements. Marketing to college students should be restricted. A 2007 study by Sallie Mae showed that more than 50 percent of college students had more than $5,000 in credit card debt while in school, and 33 percent had more than $10,000. Consumer credit has been a positive force in building a strong American economy but, like everything else in life, too much of a good thing is harmful.

A lot of this comes down to teaching young people about economics and personal finance. Parents again need to take the lead on this, but we could do a much better job in our schools as well. At the very least, economics should be included in every high school curriculum. Ideally, we would start at a much younger age. College students majoring in elementary education should be required to complete a few courses in economics so they can begin economic instruction as early as possible.

Management and Shareholders/Boards of Directors

Managers of companies need to be held accountable by experienced, independent board members who represent the interests of shareholders.

The recent explosion in top executive pay, oftentimes not related to management or stock performance, is undermining confidence in our capitalist system. It is largely due to a far-too-cozy relationship between the board of directors and the CEO. These CEOs do not put up any capital on the table, like entrepreneurs, and many have absolutely no downside risk when taking these jobs, even if they are a complete failure. In contrast, even if they completely fail to meet their objectives, they walk away from failure with generous severance packages.

Shareholder reforms are necessary to put the shareholder front and center and for shareholders to take an active role in selecting and approving board members.

Mutual and pension funds in particular represent sizable shareholder power, and they need to exercise it on the investor's behalf. We should restore the shareholders, the owners of the company, to their rightful role in selecting and overseeing a company's board and, through the board, the CEO. Here is one idea that would change the method of voting for board members. Presently, companies put up a slate of directors, and shareholders have two options: voting "yes" or "withhold." One "yes" vote is enough to get elected. This should be replaced by majority voting, where a director needs more "yes" votes than "withhold" votes.

What do General Tommy Franks, the former chief of the Public Broadcasting System, and the publisher of a Spanish newspaper have in common? They all sit on the board of Bank of America. All of them lack any financial or banking experience. So do eleven of their thirteen colleagues.

> The future of a company's top executives should be tied closely to the fortunes of the company's shareholders.

Bank of America's board members were largely picked by CEO Kenneth Lewis from several companies that it acquired as it grew into a financial giant. "This board, historically, has been viewed as a board that was there on paper," Charles M. Elson, a corporate governance expert at the University of Delaware, who owns shares in Bank of America and voted against the Merrill Lynch merger, commented in a recent interview. "But the question has been how active have they been in overseeing the CEO."

Aside from Lewis, only two people on the board—the former chief of FleetBoston and a former senior executive of MBNA—have roots in banking. How on earth could the board understand financial risks and rein in management?

This situation is hardly atypical. At Enron, where I helped develop energy projects in the Asia-Pacific region during 1994 and 1995, the situation was similar. Companies need experienced and independent board members whose interests are closely aligned with shareholders and who have access to what is going on behind the scenes in the company. The best board members are former executives who still have substantial stakes in the companies they worked for but are now independent of the CEO. These members need to be placed there by shareholders, who should be wary of CEO-picked boards.

Here are some ideas to better align the interests of corporate executives with board members and shareholders.

One problem is that state laws allow companies to create complex "advance notice" requirements that let companies derail efforts to elect shareholder-nominated board members. A legal procedure known as a poison pill, permitted under the laws of most states, effectively prohibits shareholders from accumulating a large position in a company or working with other large shareholders to influence the company. Furthermore, public corporations may legally adopt a staggered board, whereby board members are grouped into classes, with each one representing about a third of the total number of directors, so that only one class comes up for election in a year. This means it takes years and significant capital to make a significant change in the composition of a board.

Instead of being a servant, finance had become our economy's master.

A bonus plan for a CEO should be based on returns that exceed the cost of capital rather than on increases in share price or earnings per share. The awarding of restricted stock to CEOs should be quite limited, since even a small increase in share price unrelated to a CEO's performance can yield big numbers. To earn restricted stock, CEOs should have to meet tough performance goals. Vesting periods for restricted stock need to be longer than the traditional three years. Five to ten years is more appropriate, because a key goal of a CEO should be developing a management team that produces steady increases in shareholder wealth. Companies should also make their CEOs hold five to ten times their salaries in stock.

In short, the future of a company's top executives should be tied closely to the fortunes of the company's shareholders.

Industry and Finance

It may surprise you to learn that American manufacturing is alive and kicking, even though the media focuses on declining manufacturing employment numbers. The missing piece of this puzzle is the steady increase in productivity of the American worker. Interestingly, the manufacturing share of national output has stayed relatively constant at 15 percent since World War II. While services rightly lead our advanced economy, a nice balance between finance and industry is in America's best interests.

Over the past three decades, the debt of the U.S. financial sector grew six times faster than nominal GDP. The consequent increases in its scale and leverage explain why, at the peak, the financial sector generated 40 percent of American corporate profits. Incredibly, by early 2008, the market value of banking and financial shares accounted for over 30 percent of the entire U.S. stock market. From 1973 to 1985, the financial sector never earned more than 16 percent of domestic corporate profits. In 1986, that figure reached 19 percent. In the 1990s, it oscillated between 21 percent and 30 percent, higher than it had ever been in the postwar period. This decade, it reached 41 percent.

This is unhealthy: instead of being a servant, finance had become our economy's master.

It is shortsighted to think that America can keep its position in the world marketplace by drifting to a financial and service economy. Countries cannot become or stay wealthy without making stuff, too.

Manufacturing is the foundation of all wealth creation. America now has more workers in state and local governments than directly engaged in manufacturing. Many might be surprised to learn that America remains the world's largest producer of manufactured goods, although China is just a small step behind. Because of automation and technology, we need fewer workers for a given output. In January 2009, 207,000 U.S. manufacturing jobs vanished in the largest one-month drop since October 1982, and factory activity is now at a twenty-eight-year low.

Research by Mark J. Perry of the University of Michigan concludes that America remains the world's leading manufacturer by value of goods produced. Manufacturing output hit a record $1.6 trillion in 2007, and for every $1 of value produced

> Your foreign supplier today may very well be your direct competitor tomorrow.

in China's factories, America produces $2.50.

In the last thirty-seven years, manufacturing output in real dollars has more than doubled, while manufacturing employment has dropped by more than 26 percent, resulting in an almost tripling of the amount of manufacturing output per American manufacturing worker, from less than $80,000 in 1972 to almost $240,000 per worker in 2008.

It's certainly the case that the United States leads the world in overall manufacturing output, and it's probably the case that when it comes to manufacturing output per person, nobody in the world comes close to America.

Having said this, I do not mean to imply that the American worker can compete at the low end with foreign workers making a $1 an hour. Rather, we need to emulate the Japanese model: outsource the low end but ferociously defend the sophisticated high-end product manufacturing and, at the same time, protect the intellectual capital and R&D work by keeping more manufacturing at home.

This strategy is nothing new and goes way back to when America emerged on the world stage as a manufacturing power. According to League of Nations data, America's share of world manufacturing output went from 23 percent in 1870 to 35 percent in 1900 and then on to 42 percent in 1929. During this same period, Great Britain's share went from 32 percent to 9 percent.

You might think that this reversal of fortunes was due to lower wage rates in America, but you would be dead wrong. American wage rates were significantly higher than those in Britain—our edge came from investing in new machines and processes, leading to significantly higher productivity. Americans bested the mother country by looking ahead and being more effective and sophisticated capitalists. Another key was that American workers were far better educated than most workers in the world.

This is the recipe for success right now: open new overseas markets, invest in the newest technology, and improve education across the board. America needs more of a portfolio approach to manufacturing, with the low end offshore and products and research that demand constant innovation at home. A more robust trade policy, the simple tax, and cutting back excessive regulation and litigation are all part of the puzzle that will maintain and strengthen our vital manufacturing base.

Education is also critical, since our workers must be leading the way to improve quality and create new products. Smaller runs, more flexibility, and greater sophistication are the only way our manufacturing firms can grow and keep a competitive edge. No less than the former CEO of General Electric, Jack Welch, has said that American factories have to "automate, emigrate, or evaporate." I think that American manufacturing will stay strong and could begin a new surge as attitudes change.

American manufacturing executives are also learning the

hard way that having most of their manufacturing offshore is not worth the logistical headaches, labor disputes, tax and political issues, and the risk of theft of intellectual capital. Your foreign supplier today may very well be your direct competitor tomorrow. Having the flexibility to customize products and get them to domestic markets quickly is why Brooks Brothers manufactures all of its ties in Manhattan rather than overseas. This "onshoring" trend will accelerate, given the right market reforms.

One of these would be making the R&D credit permanent but there is also evidence that China's price advantage is declining due to market forces and improved productivity in America. In a recent BusinessWeek report, AlixPartners assessed the total cost of ownership of five categories of machined products, such as large, cast-aluminum engine parts requiring significant labor and small mass-produced plastic components requiring little labor. The consulting firm found there has been a dramatic cost shift since 2005.

Four years ago, the "total landed cost," meaning price after a product had arrived at a California shipping port, was 22% cheaper on average for Chinese parts than those American-made in the sample AlixPartners studied. By year-end 2008, however, the average price gap with the U.S. had dropped to only 5%, which is hardly worth all the headaches of sourcing them 7,000 miles away.

There are some signs of progress. Xerox decided in 2008 to build its first new factory in New York in two decades. Intel recently announced plans to invest $7 billion in new computer chip factories in Oregon, Arizona, and New Mexico.

Intel CEO Paul Otellini used the opportunity of a speech

before the Economic Club in Washington to vow that Intel would spend more money than ever to expand chip factories in the United States. He made that promise despite a precipitous decline in sales and profits of computer chips, the layoffs of at least 5,000 workers, and the closing of older chip plants in Asia and the United States. This is welcome news from a company that earned $11 billion in cash last year and uses its manufacturing prowess and financial strength as an edge over its rivals.

The Case for a Strong and Stable Dollar

For most of the last five years, the U.S. dollar has been weakening before recently making a surge during the economic crisis as investors sought safety in the liquidity of the American dollar. Global supply and demand will determine the value of the dollar, but American financial policy can and will influence how markets will weigh the greenback in the future.

Martin Feldstein, the chairman of the Council of Economic Advisors under President Reagan, has written that a more "competitive" or weaker U.S. dollar is good for America. I cannot overstate how strongly I believe that this opinion is incorrect. "Strong Dollar, Strong Currency" is more than a mantra for me, since economic history indicates that no country has ever achieved greatness, nor maintained it, by debasing its currency.

Have you ever heard of a country in deep economic trouble because of a strong currency? Feldstein rolls out a litany of reasons why he believes America benefits from a weaker dollar: in short, increasing exports as well as maintaining growth and employment.

Here is my case why a weaker dollar hurts America.

First, a weaker dollar translates into a cut in the real spending power of American consumers; in effect, a reduction in real income. In Europe, the number of millionaire households grew by 26.4 percent in 2007, the highest of any region in the study, helped by its strong currency against the weakening dollar. Switzerland had the top ranking for the highest density of millionaire households, with millionaire households accounting for 6.1 percent of all households.

> The value of a nation's currency reflects the perceived value of the country in the global marketplace.

Second, a weaker dollar diminishes the role of the U.S. dollar as the world's reserve currency. Why should investors and central banks around the world invest in U.S. assets when their value is steadily declining? And the Fed policy of steadily lowering interest rates compounds the problem of lowering demand for Treasury bonds and the U.S. dollar. The world's fifth-largest pension fund will no longer buy U.S. Treasury bonds because yields are too low. The move signals what could be a big shift by financial institutions away from U.S. government debt into higher-yielding assets. South Korea, whose National Pension Service has $220 billion in assets, is just one of many countries that wants to broaden its range of overseas investments.

Third, the chances of a weaker dollar leading to a sharp reduction in America's trade deficit is highly unlikely, since 40 percent of the current deficit is due to oil imports, which are denominated in U.S. dollars. An additional 20 percent is due to trade with China, which is controlling the value of its currency. A weaker dollar also hampers marketing efforts in strong currency countries because travel and lodging costs are prohibitive. One example is $600 three-star hotel rooms in many European countries. A weaker dollar may give a bump to exports short term but then, like a drug, it wears off, and we start all over again from an even weaker position.

Fourth, a weaker dollar is inflationary, since it increases the cost of imports. Just look back to the U.S. economy during the 1970s—ugly stagflation and markets going sideways year after year. I might also add that plenty of countries under IMF tutelage devalued their currencies with the hope of exporting their way out of financial trouble—name one such program that worked.

Fifth, business leaders know that discounting prices may bump near-term revenue and profits but at a real cost to long-term profitability, not to mention inflicting damage to the brand name. This is what we are doing to the brand of America by trying to increase exports by lowering their price in the global marketplace. Better to stand firm on price and sell into global markets on the basis of what is great about American products—superior quality, innovation, and service.

Sixth, investors seem to like a weaker dollar since the profits of American multinationals get a boost from foreign earnings being translated into U.S. dollars. Again, this is short-term thinking and vastly overstated, since most multinationals have sophisticated treasury departments that hedge currency exposures.

What a weaker dollar really does is to encourage American and international investors to invest in non-American markets. The more the dollar drops, the more global equities rise. A weak dollar encourages capital outflows as investors chase the momentum of higher yields and currency appreciation.

Last and perhaps most importantly, I view a policy of weakening the U.S. dollar to improve America's competitive position as the path of least resistance. Let's not roll up our sleeves and cut federal spending, greatly simplify our tax code to encourage productivity and achievement, or reduce corporate tax rates and excessive regulation. Let's just wink and weaken and let our nation's currency drift lower on automatic pilot. My view is that the value of a nation's currency reflects the perceived value of the country in the global marketplace. Maintaining and strengthening the value of our nation's currency is in the best interest of American consumers, businesses, and investors.

The Case for a Conservative Foreign Policy

By trying to save the world, could we end up losing our own country?

America tends to swing from moods of isolationism to periods when perhaps we go a bridge too far. Our approach ranges from a Nixon-Kissinger realpolitik that is too limiting to liberal interventionism through international institutions that is too expansive.

The only place to start is to ask, what is in our national

interest? Any foreign policy that is not grounded in the national interest is not sustainable, no matter how well intentioned, because it will not maintain the support of the American people.

Another approach is to view the practice of statecraft as managing the balance sheet of American resources and commitments. Walter Lippman wrote in 1943, "Foreign policy consists in bringing into balance, with a comfortable surplus of power in reserve, the nation's commitments and the nation's power."

And who could argue that our power is to a great extent based on our nation's financial resources or that, at present, our commitments strain our resources with little, if any, surplus in reserve? And this is with a 2009 defense budget of about $515 billion—

> Managing U.S. foreign policy is about managing our priorities and resources.

ten times that of the defense budget of the United Kingdom, equal to the amount spent annually by the rest of the world put together, and 4.3 percent of our $13 trillion GDP.

The Nixon doctrine essentially stated that America would support efforts by peoples around the world to gain liberty but would not supply the troops. The Reagan doctrine can be described as containment plus. It relied on strengthened deterrence, incremental pressure, soaring rhetoric, and opportunistic and limited intervention to bring down the Soviet empire without firing a shot or directly confronting Soviet power. In short, it was a reflective and conservative approach to foreign affairs rather than pursuing a policy of reflexive intervention.

My view is that President Reagan got it just about right by balancing realistic goals with resources and understanding that the threat of force needed to be tied to aggressive diplomacy. He also was keenly aware that military and political power was dependent on economic power. In addition, while he was ideologically aggressive in spreading freedom and democracy, with big goals, such as toppling the Soviet empire and blowing holes through the Iron Curtain, his administration moved carefully, building a strong and enduring base of public support.

Marginal gains were welcome, and risks were weighed against goals and resources. Constant and persistent pressure was brought to bear, with incremental gains cascading to the fall of the Berlin Wall. Professor Henry Nau of George Washington University recently published an excellent article in *The Public Interest* on this topic entitled "Conservative Internationalism."

One key issue is the importance of timing. President Reagan waited to confront the Soviets until the U.S. economy rebounded from the deep recession in the early 1980s and after our military buildup became a reality. A wise foreign policy is opportunistic and alert to developments around the world that could lead to commercial or ideological gains. The Louisiana Purchase and the Solidarity movement in Poland are examples of just such historic diplomatic breakthroughs.

I accept America's role in spreading openness, prosperity, freedom, self-government, and the respect for the dignity of each individual around the world, but I also recognize that there are limits to what we can achieve. These limits include resources, public opinion, and the probability of success weighed against the costs of failure. Best-case scenarios need to be treated with skepticism, while worst-case scenarios cannot be ignored.

There is no virtue in extremes. Sometimes, we need to act forcefully to protect our vital interests in a confrontational manner. Other times, we might heed the credo of the dexterous Victorian age Prime Minister Salisbury, who mused that "British policy is to drift lazily downstream, occasionally putting out a boat-hook to avoid a collision."

The power of America's example is perhaps our most effective tool of fostering change in the world. I am both an ardent nationalist and an eyes-open internationalist. It should be clear that we have global interests and threats, and we have to compete successfully in the global economic arena to increase our prosperity.

We need to react aggressively to direct material threats to our national interest, but the threat and use of force should be married to diplomacy. Constant attention should be directed at building public opinion to support foreign policy goals and to build strong partnerships with like-minded countries.

One reason for a prudent approach to armed intervention is that no matter how thorough the war planning and how skillful the execution, war brings to the table a high degree of uncertainty. Worst-case scenarios come to life more often than best-case scenarios.

Sir Winston Churchill, no shrinking violet when it came to conflict or using force, stated that "the statesman who yields to war fever is no longer the master of policy, but the slave of unforeseen and unacceptable events." Carl von Clausewitz, the dean of war strategy, freely admitted, "War is the realm of chance."

Managing U.S. foreign policy is about managing our priorities and resources. Specifically, our priorities need to be adjusted to reflect the changing center of gravity in world markets and power. The battles against radical Islam, terrorism, and nuclear proliferation have to stay at the top of our agenda, but we need to also focus more on economic issues and opening overseas markets.

America needs to rebalance its focus, attention, and resources on emerging markets in Asia and our own hemisphere. Our country's future lies more with Brazil than with France and, perhaps, more with Southeast Asia than with Germany. The attitude of wise man and former Secretary of State Dean Acheson that viewed Asia as a mere distraction to Europe have been costly and have to end. Despite clear evidence of Asia's growing importance, America's foreign policy establishment is still too Eurocentric. While national security must always be our top priority, more attention needs to be directed to expanding global economic and commercial opportunities. Asia represents 48 percent of the world's population, with heavyweights such as Japan, China, and India. Add to this the 850 million people and $1 trillion-plus GDP from ASEAN countries, including Indonesia, the world's largest Muslim country.

This part of the world highlights the importance of the oceans to world commerce and security. More than 90 percent of all global goods and 65 percent of oil travels by sea. Americans have a tendency to focus on the Atlantic and Pacific oceans at the expense of the third-largest body of water in the world: the Indian Ocean. Spanning seven time zones, the Indian Ocean will likely be a key backdrop in the early twenty-first century. Keep in mind that China and India represent, after America, the next two largest navies in the world, and 40 percent of world trade passes through the Straits of Malacca chokepoint. Countries such as India, Malaysia, and Indonesia may seem like faraway places to most Americans, but they will loom increasingly larger in the coming decades.

We also have to deepen our relationship with Japan in economic, cultural, and security matters. Despite the growth of China and India, Japan should remain the cornerstone of our Asian strategy. Next comes promoting closer security, economic, and trade relations with India and revitalizing our involvement with ASEAN members. Of particular interest is doing what we can to strengthen democracy and economic cooperation with Indonesia, located in a strategically vital part of the world. China's "string of pearls" strategy whereby it has developed ports and posts throughout south Asia is causing disquiet in India. Interestingly, China announced plans to construct an aircraft carrier while India recently launched its first nuclear-powered submarine.

> Hoping for the best is not a sound China policy.

We also need to pay closer attention to our hemisphere. Mexico is a good example. There is currently an escalating drug war going on near the U.S.-Mexican border. Driven by corruption and violence, it could easily spin out of control, leading to a mass exodus. While we gain control over our border, expanding American exports to Latin America, particularly to Brazil, warrants a major effort and commitment of resources.

The balance between isolationism and constant intervention has to be based on good judgement and common sense. While many in Europe bemoan our active engagement in world affairs, Former UK Prime Minister Tony Blair had it right when he addressed a joint session of the Australian Parliament on March 27, 2006: "The great danger with America today is not that they are too much involved. The danger is that they decide to pull up the drawbridge and disengage."

Finally, it is important to note that trust is the "coin of the realm" when it comes to both domestic and international politics. If America is considered by some to be an empire, it is built on trust rather than on commerce or conquest.

A Realistic China Policy

Hoping for the best is not a sound China policy. Next to the conflict with radical Islam, there is no more important foreign policy issue than understanding and dealing with the challenge and opportunity presented by China.

A clear and consistent China policy, coupling maximum cooperation with realistic expectations, is essential. Our China policy needs to be pragmatic and hard headed. While we certainly hope that China's often-quoted "peaceful development" and "harmonious society" comes to pass, we must also recognize the Chinese adage, "prosperous country, strong army." China's defense budget is growing at the fastest rate in the world, and soon it will spend more each year on its military than all the nations in the European Union combined. It also has the largest army in the world.

The annual report from the Defense Department to Congress, *Military Power of the People's Republic of China 2009,* describes efforts by China to supply its armed forces with weapons that can be used to intimidate and attack Taiwan and deal with the superiority of American naval and air power, at least near its territory. The Pentagon report describes how China's military modernization has continued, with a particular focus on Taiwan, which China considers a renegade province. China has built up short-range missiles across from Taiwan, even though relations between the two have improved some-what over the past year.

To blunt traditional advantages of the United States, China is developing new technologies for cyber and space warfare, in addition to sustaining and modernizing its nuclear arsenal, according to the report. The Chinese military also is expand-ing and improving its fleet of submarines and hopes to build a number of new aircraft carriers.

The opening paragraph of this report's executive summary sums up the situation well:

> China's rapid rise as a regional political and economic power with growing global influence has significant implications for the Asia-Pacific region and the world. The United States welcomes the rise of a stable, peaceful, and prosperous China, and encourages China to participate responsibly in world affairs by taking on a greater share of the

burden for the stability, resilience, and growth of the international system. The United States has done much over the last thirty years to encourage and facilitate China's national development and its integration into the international system. However, much uncertainty surrounds China's future course, particularly regarding how its expanding military power might be used.

While we have spent, during the last seven years, close to $1 trillion in Iraq, China has amassed $2 trillion in foreign exchange reserves, built a world-class infrastructure, and sharply escalated its armed forces. U.S. National Intelligence Director Dennis Blair recently testified to Congress that the Chinese have become assertive in staking claims to international waters around economic zones and were "more aggressive and forward-looking than we saw a couple of years before" in Southeast Asia and the South China Sea. The South China Sea has some of the world's busiest shipping lanes, since it is the shortest route between the Pacific and Indian oceans. Over half of the globe's oil tanker traffic passes through the sea, which is also said to hold valuable fishing grounds, and lucrative and unexploited oil and natural gas fields.

You have to ask yourself, has China been the major beneficiary of America's preoccupation with Iraq, Afghanistan, and the Middle East? How much has it contributed to helping America in the global war on terror? How long will China block progress on a host of issues, from Iran to Sudan, using its permanent seat on the United Nations Security Council?

In 1788, the American ship *Empress of China* set sail from

New York for Canton. Since then, America has been captivated with penetrating China's potentially enormous consumer markets. The unfortunate reality is that China exports to America five times more than it imports.

Then there was the recent Chinese government rejection, on competition grounds, of Coca-Cola's proposed $2.4 billion takeover of the country's leading juice maker. People familiar with the matter said the ministry's thinking reflected wider worries in Beijing about the loss of a leading brand to a foreign company. This indefensible decision came right on the heels of Coca-Cola opening a $90 million innovation and technology center in Shanghai and pledging to invest $2 billion in China by 2012. Something is wrong with this picture.

While Chinese companies operate freely in the private enterprise global economy, most of the Chinese economy and certainly the leading companies remain in state hands.

Meanwhile, China's goal is quite straightforward and clear to me: to maintain Chinese Communist party rule and political stability, sustain economic growth, defend Chinese sovereignty, and restore China's status as a great power. To achieve these goals, it needs to build a strong economy and military and gradually weaken the role of America and Japan in the Asia-Pacific region.

That China has these ambitions would not be cause for concern if it were an open, pluralistic, democratic, and private enterprise country. But it is not, and despite the belief of many policymakers hoping for reforms, China is unlikely to move toward meaningful reform in any of these areas. The reason is that the Chinese Communist party's overriding goal is to maintain power while it seeks to achieve hegemony in Asia. The outcome of China's cocktail of limited economic freedom blended with political repression is uncertain at best.

Over the past quarter century, no country has gained more from globalization than China. While Chinese companies operate freely in the private enterprise global economy, most of the Chinese economy and certainly the leading companies remain in state hands. When I served on the board of the Asian Development Bank during the early 1990s, I repeatedly called for China to privatize its companies, but this call was met by rejoinders from most board members, describing me as the "impatient young American." Here we are almost two decades later, and 34 of the top 35 companies and 75 percent of the largest 1,500 companies listed on the Shanghai Stock Exchange are still owned or controlled by the Chinese government. It is the Chinese that are patiently grinding us down.

We do need to work with the Chinese when we can but also accept that China played a key role in derailing the latest round of world trade talks. Religious and political freedom, a free press, and an open media and society are seen as a direct threat to its power and stability.

America needs to accept these truths and form a realistic China policy that protects its interests and stands on the side of freedom, reform, and private enterprise. Right now, the commercial challenge from China is on the front burner. We need to use the principle of reciprocity to open more markets in China for American firms. The window to use our superior leverage due to the size of our consumer markets is closing fast, and the Chinese realize this. The longer they can stall and delay, the better their negotiating stance.

China is already the third-largest economy in the world, with the third-largest military budget. HSBC Bank projects that China could surge past Japan to become the world's second largest economy as early as 2010. It is using its growing clout to expand its relationships with and selling arms to America's adversaries in Africa and the Middle East. A Sino-Russian alliance is blossoming, while China is deepening commercial alliances in America's backyard, Latin America. In early 2009, the United States lodged a formal protest with the government in Beijing after five Chinese ships harassed an American surveillance vessel in international waters, in actions the Pentagon described as "illegal, unprofessional, and dangerous."

America needs to cooperate with China whenever possible, seek more transparency and open communications, and develop commercial opportunities on a reciprocal basis. It also needs to be mindful of the advice of China's former paramount leader Deng Xiaoping, in the early 1990s, to his country: "Observe calmly; secure our position; cope with affairs calmly; hide our capacities and bide our time; be good at maintaining a low profile; and never claim leadership."

In short, friendly but firm should be our approach to China. Firm in our convictions and firm in protecting our strategic and economic interests.

- *The Importance of Intelligence and Speaking Truth to Power*

Finally, the importance of timely intelligence and speaking truth to power are critical to America's security. David Halberstam puts in well in his history of the Korean War, *The Coldest Winter*:

> The importance and value of good, independent intelligence men in wartime can hardly be overemphasized. A great intelligence officer studies the unknown and works in the darkness, trying to see the shape of future events. He covers the sensitive ground where prejudice, or instinctive cultural bias, often meet reality, and he must stand for reality, even if it means standing virtually alone.

Sun Tzu describes the importance of intelligence even more forcefully in the last paragraph of *The Art of War*: "Hence it is only the enlightened ruler and the wise general who will use the highest intelligence of the army for the purposes of spying, and thereby they achieve great results."

- *America's Role as a Global Philanthropic Superpower*

Americans are the most generous people in the world in donating their money, time, and talent to philanthropic organizations. In 2007, Americans donated $300 billion, with 76 percent coming from individuals who, on average, donated 2.2 percent of their income.

By most measures, Americans remain the most charitable people worldwide. In 2007, giving in the United States aver-aged 1.75 percent of gross domestic product, according to the Charities Aid Foundation, compared to 0.75 percent in Britain. In Germany, France, and Singapore, the rate of giving was about 0.25 percent of GDP last year. Unfortunately, rather than softening the face of American power, this generosity is neither understood nor appreciated by the world.

The great majority of private charitable organizations are well run, cost-effective, and entrepreneurial. They are also experts in their specialties and close to the people they are trying to help. Perhaps the fastest-growing aid providers are religious organizations, which heed the 2,000 verses in the good book on helping the poor. These spiritually based groups are also increasingly global in their mission. Minister Rick Warren identifies five global giants to overcome: spiritual emptiness, selfish leadership, hunger, sickness, and illiteracy.

All contributions to these organizations should be tax exempt, and government organizations whose missions overlap with private charities should allow them to lead and manage programs, limiting their role to matching private contributions.

One example is the U.S. Agency for International Development (USAID), which has an annual budget of about $10 billion. Rather than fund and try to manage development projects all over the world, let's use this USAID money to match funds raised by private American foundations and charitable organizations.

According to Giving USA, about $100 billion of American charitable contributions were for global causes, such as economic development, medical research, and disaster assistance. Global aid projects can be run much more efficiently by charitable organizations, and the goodwill generated by these organizations as they help people around the globe will transform America's image abroad. As the breadbasket of the world, America is also in a position to distribute food to more than 800 million of the world's 6 billion people, who are unable to obtain the adequate, nutritious food needed for sound health and growth.

Such undernourishment negatively affects people's health and productivity. According to the World Health Organization, poor nutrition causes one in three people to die prematurely or have disabilities. Among young children, the impact is even greater—malnutrition is a contributing factor in more than 50 percent of deaths among children under the age of five worldwide.

The potential exists to use American agricultural surpluses to greatly expand the American Red Cross's nutrition initiatives. For example, in Vietnam, about half of elementary schoolchildren are malnourished. Providing food in school to students every day, as well as take-home food rations to families of students, acts as an incentive for children to attend school. The take-home ration, while also nutritious, helps offset families' financial expenditures on food.

America can lead a revolution in entrepreneurial philanthropy at home and around the globe. As Bill Clinton rightly points out in *Giving*, talent in terms of intelligence and energy is spread evenly across the world but the capital and organizations needed to create opportunity are lacking. The goal of America's aid activities should be to close this opportunity gap.

A Forward-Leaning Trade Policy

America's free trade-versus-protectionism debate needs to be recast.

Just as there is no free trade, only fringe elements want to wall off the world. To maintain a robust growth rate, we must open markets for our goods and services, and we can do this if we just leverage our huge consumer markets and negotiate more advantageous trade accords.

The rise of Asia and, in particular, China presents America with the largest economic challenge in its history. On the economic front, China's substantial low-cost advantage, economies of scale, and entrepreneurial energy translate into extreme competitive pressure on America's companies, workers, and industrial base. Our trade deficit with China alone was $266 billion in 2008, and the China Central Bank is financing almost 30 percent of our budget deficit by purchasing U.S. Treasury bonds. In addition, the great majority of leading Chinese companies are state-owned or controlled.

It is not protectionist to use the leverage of our huge consumer market to open markets on a reciprocal basis. No one wants to go back to the 1929–1934 period, when world trade plunged by more than 60 percent, but America's most important asset in negotiating trade and economic agreements is our huge consumer market.

While participating in global trade organizations, we should not hesitate to negotiate advantageous bilateral trade agreements. A major goal should be to open global agricultural, consumer, and financial markets to American products and services. American exports support one out of five U.S. manufacturing jobs, and jobs tied directly to exports pay 13 percent to 18 percent higher than other jobs. America is also well positioned to expand its agricultural exports that now account for about 30 percent of our total agricultural output. Agricultural exports now account for 925,000 American jobs.

The Chinese are using just the hope of accessing their consumer market to force American and European multinationals to manufacture in China, share intellectual capital, and invest in Chinese projects. We already have the market but do not use the enormous negotiating leverage we have in our hands.

Even in our own backyard we are losing market share to the Chinese. Bilateral trade between China and Latin America has increased an amazing 10-fold since 2000 and in 2009, China passed America as Brazil's largest trade partner. From Chilean copper to Brazilian iron ore, China has emerged as the biggest buyer.

Another top priority must be to protect our hard-earned intellectual property rights and capital. If countries continue to tolerate the rampant theft of intellectual property and counterfeiting, we should consider penalties, such as tariffs on imports, as a form of compensation. A fair principle of economic relations with other countries is reciprocity. If U.S. consumer markets are open to a country's exports, American exports must have free access to their markets. If overseas private companies can invest freely in American companies and capital markets, American firms should have similar privileges. The policy of mercantilism by some of our trading partners is weakening our economic base and undermining American support for open markets.

Part Three

Renewing America's Promise and Prosperity

So far, we have learned the reasons why America is special and the challenges to our economic and political leadership, both at home and abroad. Now we come to the proverbial fork in the road. What is the next chapter in the American story? Will we come out of the current financial turbulence a stronger, more prosperous nation, or will we make the wrong choices, leading to relative decline? To frame this issue, we will look first at the lessons from Japan taking the wrong road.

Next, we will look at the right blueprint for economic recovery, based on the beliefs and actions of the founding partners of America Inc., George Washington and Alexander Hamilton, as well as Abraham Lincoln, the founder of the Republican party. Finally, we will recap the themes of this book with an ambitious "why not?" agenda for America that will renew America's promise and prosperity.

• *Japan's Surprising Fall*

> *Washington must not go down the rough road traveled by Japan.*
>
> —*Asahi Shimbun* editorial of March 4, 2009

Japan and the Japanese economy were riding high in the 1980s, building on the country's remarkable resurgence since its devastating defeat in World War II. The bestseller *Japan Is #1* was the talk of the town, companies around the world were rattled by seemingly invincible Japanese companies like Sony, and congressmen were clamoring for protectionist legislation.

David Halberstam included in his book *The Next Century* part of a speech he gave in early 1989 before the governors of the fifty states of the Union:

> If there were any purely economic model for the future, it was the Japanese. They were a fierce and relentless competitor; it was now quite possible that they were setting the standards for other nations in terms of being a well-educated, industrious, disciplined society.

Later that very year, the Tokyo stock market hit its apogee, and then things fell apart. A banking crisis, combined with a real estate meltdown, led to a sharp and prolonged recession and the much-talked-about "Lost Decade." The banking system failed to aggressively confront its bad loans, in an attempt to put off the inevitable pain. Politicians avoided tough choices and launched a series of ten infrastructure stimulus packages that, in turn, led to a staggering national debt equal to 180 percent of the country's GDP. The cross-share ownership of Japanese companies, a source of strength and stability during the boom, became an albatross.

In 2009, Japan's broad TOPIX market index fell to a level reached in 1984, wiping out a quarter of a century of gains. Japan's stock market value is roughly one third the peak of nearly two decades ago, and its GDP is at 1996 levels. The Nikkei stock index has collapsed to where it stands today: at one fifth the value it had attained in 1989. Once-dominating multinationals began defaulting on loans, and many went out of business entirely. Individuals couldn't repay their debts. Real estate values fell dramatically and today remain as much as 50 percent below their 1989 peak. People simply turned over the keys to their homes and disappeared in the dark of the night. Sound familiar?

Avoiding the Fate of Japan

The similarities between what Japan faced and what America confronts today is unnerving: in short, undercapitalized banks, high levels of debt, and weak consumer spending. The cumulative total of bank losses on bad debt between 1993 and 2005 in Japan reached a punishing 20 percent of GDP.

I was an overseas college student in Japan at Sophia University and Keio University in the early 1980s, and I covered Tokyo for an investment bank, so the Japan story for me is real and personal. Why and how did Japan come unraveled? Did it not still have the competitive advantages of a strong work ethic, a world-class education system, and capable corporate leaders well respected for their dedication and teamwork?

After much reflection, I have decided that there are a number of reasons for Japan's economic morass. It is a bit different from the conventional wisdom that Japan responded too slowly to the crisis or that it was the result of a series of policy blunders by Japan's vaunted technocrats. We need to dig deeper to get at the cultural reasons for Japan's collective loss of confidence.

> We need to dig deeper to get at the cultural reasons for Japan's collective loss of confidence.

First, when a country has a head of economic momentum, when the wind is at its back, many shortcomings can be put aside to be dealt with another day. For Japan, this was the cozy cross-holdings of shares, which tied its great industrial groups together, normally with a large bank at its core. As the economy and share prices declined, these arrangements proved to be too inflexible to adapt.

Japan's politics was also deeply entrenched, and the ruling Liberal Democratic party's (LDP's) incredibly close ties to corporate interests prevented it from acting independently and aggressively. Only a brief respite, during the leadership of Prime Minister Junichiro Koizumi from 2001 to 2006, breathed some fresh air and initiative into Japanese politics. That this was the time when Japanese markets rebounded seems no coincidence to me.

Japan's political system has proven to be a major handicap in reacting to its reversal of fortunes. Karel Van Wolferen in *The Enigma of Japanese Power* vividly describes how there is no ultimate leader or power center that can take decisive action. The one-party dominance of Japan's Liberal Democratic party is also an illusion, since it has relied on many conflicting constituencies in order to win elections. In short, there is no place in Japan where, as Harry Truman put it, "the buck stops."

Most importantly, as it sank in that a quick economic recovery was not in the cards, Japan incrementally lost its confidence. The swagger of the 1980s was replaced by a downcast attitude of survival. The Japanese financial system became known for its "zombie" banks, Japanese families hoarded cash and invested overseas, and Japanese companies were preoccupied with cutting costs rather than expanding domestic markets. The rise of China accelerated Japan's loss of self-confidence.

While expanding exports to China and America gave the Japanese economy some life, the current global slowdown has crippled its growth prospects. The Japanese economy is suffering its worst economic contraction in thirty-five years and a recession that may be the worst in fifty years. According to Japan's Ministry of Finance, the country's industrial production and exports may fall 30 percent, and its GDP could drop as much as 10 percent in 2009. Toyota is experiencing its first losses since 1938, as every digit of yen appreciation results in an additional $450 million in operating losses.

America is an Asia-Pacific country and needs to keep the "no limits" attitude so pervasive in emerging market countries.

Hiroko Tabuchi reports that all of this accumulated negative news has destroyed consumer confidence and unleashed a sea change in consumer attitudes. Between 2001 and 2007, per-capita consumer spending rose only a minuscule 0.2 percent. Here are just some indications of Japanese miserly ways: Many use old bath water to do laundry, sales of whiskey have fallen to a fifth of their peak, and car sales have fallen by half since 1990.

"Japan is so dependent on exports that when overseas markets slow down, Japan's economy teeters on collapse," said Hideo Kumano, an economist at the Dai-Ichi Life Research Institute. "On the surface, Japan looked like it had recovered from its Lost Decade of the 1990s. But Japan in fact entered a second Lost Decade—that of lost consumption."

In contrast to traditional lifetime employment, about a third of the Japanese labor force has been transformed into temporary workers who have no job security and fewer benefits. Japan's aging population also poses a considerable headwind for its economy. Retiring baby boomers are just not spending as expected. Japan's population has been falling since 2005, and its working-age population could fall by a third by mid-century. There are 18 million babies born in China each year, compared to 1.1 million in Japan.

The Japanese are also becoming poorer, relatively speaking: Japan's per-capita income, once among the top five in the world, slipped to nineteenth in 2007, far behind the United States and many European countries.

There are some clear lessons for America here. How can we make sure we do not follow the sad story of Japan's collective loss of confidence leading to a no-growth economy?

There are some who argue that Japan's imbalances were much larger than those that have developed in America. From 1981 to 1991, commercial land prices in Japan's six largest cities rose 500 percent. From 1996 to 2006, housing prices in America's twenty largest cities rose 200 percent. America's debt problem for nonfinancial companies is not nearly as acute as in Japan. For every dollar of corporate debt, there are two dollars of net worth for American firms. In Japan, there were three dollars of corporate debt for just one dollar of equity.

It is also true that the American government has reacted more quickly and forcefully to try to address the crisis, bringing benchmark interest rates to zero and using public funds to recapitalize banks. It took Japan nine years to bring rates to zero and eight years to use public funds to shore up "zombie" banks. (On the other hand, Japan fell apart when the rest of the world was rather robust. Now we are trying to right our economic ship in a stormy sea of global financial turmoil.) Finally, Japan made a crucial error in 1997 when it raised taxes after the Japanese economy finally found some traction.

It seems to me that America also has a number of advantages over Japan that should help us react and recover more quickly. Our economy and society are more open and flexible. We have in the past more readily accepted creative destruction, whereby failing companies are replaced by new ones. In Japan, the nail that sticks out gets hammered down. In America, they start new companies.

And our grassroots political system can force big and difficult change on its legislative leaders. Will the American people have the courage and energy to come together and demand the changes we need to put the country on a higher growth trajectory?

It is not all that complicated, but it will require significant will and action. Above all, we need to resist the twin evils of trimming our expectations and expanding our reliance on government. I have no doubt that the prolonged weakness of Japan is due primarily to a loss of confidence in its future. It is psychology, not economics, that has put Japan's economy back to where it was twenty-five years ago: an inability to change, a resistance to trying something new, a running away from risk, a yearning for security over growth, a hesitancy to open Japan's closed society. All of this has led to a paralysis of Japan's economic and political system.

In addition, there is a growing Japanese tendency to look backwards rather than thinking forward. Rather than making the changes required to get back on a higher economic growth trajectory, Japan seems instead to be looking backward for comfort and forward with resignation, rather than optimism.

Growing with Asian and Emerging Markets

If America pursues frugality without growth, we will become

another Japan. A pro-growth approach means changing our attitude from one of just trying to compete with Asian and emerging market countries to one of growing with them. America is an Asia-Pacific country and needs to keep the "no limits" attitude so pervasive in emerging market countries.

I founded America Unbound, an economic strategy think tank, to focus in on this mission because, quite frankly, there is no other alternative to fostering the 4 percent to 5 percent consistent economic growth America needs to pay down our debt and fund our commitments.

Let's for a moment compare prospects in more developed markets with the tremendous opportunities in emerging markets.

According to the United Nations' median estimates, between now and the middle of the next century, the world population will most likely increase by some 3.68 billion people, and all of this increase will be contributed by emerging countries. Between 1995 and 2025, Asia's population will grow by 1.35 billion. Today, Europe and Africa are each home of about 12 percent of the world population. Europe's share of the global population will shrink to about 6.8 percent in 2050. Africa's share will grow to 21.8 percent.

According to a March 1, 2009, article in *The Wall Street Journal,* "In the next twenty-four hours, approximately 180,000 people in developing countries will be moving from the countryside to cities such as Shanghai, São Paulo, and Johannesburg. The same will happen tomorrow and every day thereafter for the next thirty years." This represents 65.7 million new urban consumers every year, equal to a new New York City every two months.

Alexander Green notes that Western markets are relatively mature, since there are already 900 cars for every 1,000 people in the United States, over 96.5 percent of U.S. workers are already connected to the Internet using broadband connections, and 26 million fewer cell phones will be sold in Europe this year than in 2007.

Meanwhile, each year, 75 million people from emerging markets join the global middle class, and if current trends hold, by 2030, 90 percent of the world's middle class consumers will reside in emerging nations, controlling over $6 trillion in disposable income.

General Motors has a 9 percent market share in China, where 25,000 more cars hit the road every day. About 15 million new cell phone subscribers will sign up every year in India this year, and that is more new users each month than the entire population of Dallas.

Technology and communications is feeding this growth, and by 2012 there may be 2 billion new computer users in Africa, Latin America, Asia, and Eastern Europe. Argentina's number of Internet users has gone up 700 percent since 2000, and yet only 6.4 percent of the population currently has broadband access. China alone consumes a third of the world's steel, and in the next few years, it plans to build ninety-seven new airports and spend $292 billion on railways.

This very brief overview of growth prospects in Asia and emerging markets should have all American companies dusting off their strategic plans to refocus them on tapping into these profitable opportunities. This is a promise that we must spaciously fulfill.

• *Keeping Faith in America's Promise*

In 1941, the influential *Life* magazine proclaimed "the American century," but it is unlikely you will see this sentiment widely expressed in today's media circles. Many Americans seem to have the dual emotions of concern and skepticism about their country's position in the world, as well as about its future.

With this, an interesting shift has subsequently taken place: Americans increasingly viewed the federal government as a "savior of last resort" and became thankful of the efforts by lawmakers to deal with the economic downturn. Americans even grew irritable when some commentators and leaders had the temerity to criticize those bailout and stimulus programs. There was clearly a feeling that, while the bailout and stimulus were far from perfect, at least Washington was trying to do something.

This mood was captured well by Columbia University historian Kenneth T. Jackson, who commented, "There is a shifting of power and influence at the moment from Manhattan to Washington. The same thing happened during other financial crises in our history but most especially in the 1930s."

We need to go back to our very beginning—to what made the American economy the envy of the world in the first place. Reverse the trend toward a more complicated tax code and higher tax rates; cut rather than expand regulations and red tape; rein in spending and begin paying off our national debt; reward saving, investment, and risk taking; reduce health care costs; shift more responsibility to individuals; and expand overseas markets.

We also need to unclog our political system by forcing Congress to be fiscally responsible and giving more power to citizens at the local and state level. Government needs to trim its sails and keep in mind its purpose of helping Americans reach their full potential rather than impeding progress and opportunity. We need to go back to the beliefs and principles of the architects of America.

Following the Blueprint of Washington, Hamilton, and Lincoln

Going back to our Founding Fathers brings us to the critical partnership between George Washington and Alexander Hamilton. Without these founding partners working together in harness, our country could have easily taken a less successful path. Let's look a bit closer at their complementary personalities and how their lives and values highlight many of the themes presented in this book.

While I worked with the U.S. Congress and U.S. Treasury in Washington, one of my favorite destinations was Mount Vernon. Oftentimes, I spent the whole day there, exploring every nook and cranny of this great farming estate. Here George Washington's personality comes alive, and it is a far cry from the wooden, stiff image of his portraits.

Washington was an entrepreneurial and practical man. His father's death prevented him from getting any more than an elementary education, but throughout his life, he strove to improve and educate himself by independent study. He loved the outdoors, choosing at age thirteen the craft of a surveyor. This bred a lifelong appetite for land and wealth. Adventure, ambition, and exploration fueled his decision to combine a military career with acquiring and managing property. Today,

> Above all, George Washington demonstrated good judgment throughout his career.

he might be called a real estate tycoon, but he considered himself a gentleman farmer.

After renowned service in the French and Indian War, Washington devoted his prodigious energies to Mount Vernon, which was bequeathed to him by his half-brother Lawrence's wife. From that time, Mount Vernon became his home and the heart of his life. His goal was to make it a profitable and self-sustaining enterprise, and this reflected his own self-reliant, independent personality. One constant irritant was his reliance on British capital and trade through Cary & Company, which bought his crops and imported European goods for the estate. Washington bristled at this uncomfortable dependence, and this was one reason he avidly sought and supported American independence.

He was a great innovator and experimented with all sorts of agricultural and breeding practices. Rather than follow the norm of one staple crop, such as tobacco, Washington diversified into wheat, rye, peas, and potatoes and was way ahead of his time in terms of conservation and land use, by using crop rotation and searching for ways to make his land yield more per acre. Everything produced at Mount Vernon was used, with little waste and no patience for slovenly work. Nets groaning with shad were pulled from the Potomac, and he traded his goods all over the world. Although Washington liked a glass of fine Spanish Madeira with his simple but ample dinners, he built the largest whiskey distillery in America right at Mount Vernon.

He was no stay-in-the-office type of manager. Up before dawn, after some time catching up on his correspondence and his usual repast of hot cakes swimming in butter and syrup, he jumped on his horse and spent the next six hours touring his farm and supervising projects. He was a taskmaster but was not above jumping in to help with a spade or ax. While he was, without question, an accomplished practical businessman, he loved sporting pursuits, and Jefferson called him the finest horseman in all of Virginia.

Washington also appreciated the concept of balance, especially in architecture and gardening. He studied both subjects closely and took great pride in applying the most modern methods. His life was a testament to independent study and lifelong learning, as he read twelve newspapers each day and built a fine library. His vision of America's future was anything but small, and he was keenly interested in exploring and settling western lands and finding ways to improve navigation and transportation. Washington dreamed of an America expanding and growing commercial markets westward and recognized that Britain was determined to block and control this growth.

As commander and later as president, Washington constantly referred to the need for national unity. At his first headquarters near Boston, he saw that militias and political leaders owed their primary allegiance to their states and sought to shift the focus to national unity and pride. In his farewell address, he dwelt on the issue of unity with both passion and foreboding.

All these beliefs and characteristics served him well as he assumed the role as our nation's first president. President Washington saw his role as establishing the precedents and setting the stage for America's growth and prosperity. Above all, George Washington demonstrated good judgment throughout his career, and as Alexander Hamilton observed, he "resolved slowly, resolved surely." He was also an excellent judge of talent and got more than what even he probably expected from his brilliant and bold aide-de-camp and de facto chief of staff, Alexander Hamilton.

• *"A Host Unto Himself"*

Alexander Hamilton's life is a quintessential story of American mobility, merit, and ambition. He was an ardent nationalist and capitalist, a daring military leader and strategist, the principal author of *The Federalist Papers*, and one of the key architects of the American political and economic system. He represented that rare breed of leaders, being both a thinker and a doer.

Hamilton's beginnings were humble and humiliating. Abandoned by his father and losing his mother to illness, he and his brother were largely alone in the world. His portable library became his most loyal companion. He was largely self-educated, until a group of businessmen noticed his literary and business talents and sent him to what is now Columbia University in New York. His journey from the tiny island of Nevis in the British West Indies to St. Croix and subsequent emigration to colonial America is a testament to the need for us to remain open to immigration. Imagine not allowing someone with Alexander Hamilton's gifts into America!

Hamilton's rise was based on merit rather than connections to the crown. He caught the eye of General Washington as an impossibly young officer commanding an artillery unit and soon was invited to join General Washington's "family," where he made himself indispensable. One of the themes threading through Hamilton's career was his call for "energy in the executive." This was his calling card throughout his life as well.

During the Constitutional Convention and the battle for ratification, he played an instrumental role as the leading author of *The Federalist Papers* and proved his mettle as a persuasive and agile New York politico. Then came the crown of his career, as our nation's first treasury secretary. You may think that the challenge of dealing with the current financial turbulence is unprecedented, but you would be wrong.

As he took command of the Treasury Department, the new nation's finances were in disarray. There was no central bank, the war debt was enormous, each state had its own currency, there was little if any federal revenue, and in the first place most states did not want much of a central government at all. Undaunted, Secretary Hamilton jumped into the breach with all cylinders firing. In short order, the wheels were in motion for a budget and tax system, a mint, a central bank and customs service, a coast guard, and a strategy to make America a commercial empire on par with the glittering capitals of Europe.

Although 95 percent of Americans tilled the soil at this time, Secretary Hamilton envisioned an economic balance between agriculture and industry, and his *Report on Manufactures* set forth a strategy to achieve this goal. This controversial strategy was challenged by cabinet rival and Anglophobe Thomas Jefferson, who wanted America to remain largely an agrarian society. Hamilton also added the third dimension of finance and understood its pivotal role in fueling and lubricating industrial growth, outlined in his *Report on Public Credit.* The growing role of corporations, shareholders, and management in America's emerging economy was welcomed and fostered by his policies and personal involvement.

Hamilton's goal of a more independent and self-reliant economy was sharpened by his wartime experience. He stated that "a free people" ought to "promote manufactories such as to render them independent of others for essential, particularly for military, supplies." Secretary Hamilton's ability to dominate the first cabinet was not only due to his energy, creativity, and decisiveness but also because President Washington shared his vision for America. The president grasped the basic elements of the Hamiltonian plan while the treasury chief managed the complexities.

The speed at which his proposals moved forward staggered his critics, as Jefferson proclaimed him to be "a host unto himself." Just take a look at Secretary Hamilton's initiatives, during 1789–1794, which formed the very foundation and institutional underpinnings of the American economy:

- Submits to Congress his *Report on Public Credit*, which forms the basis for consolidating and managing the national debt and incorporates a plan to eliminate the nation's public debt in thirty years.

- Negotiates, over a dinner with Thomas Jefferson and James Madison, the deal to move the nation's capital to the Potomac in exchange for support for Hamilton's debt policies.

- Receives authorization from Congress to create a service to enforce customs laws, which would become the Coast Guard.

- Submits a report arguing for establishment of a central bank, leading to formation of the Bank of the United States.

- Delivers a report calling for creation of a national mint and defining the U.S. dollar in quantities of gold and silver.

- Directs purchases of government securities to stabilize markets.

- Submits the *Report on Manufactures*, setting forth a strategy to transform the country into an industrial power.

- Manages a panic and crisis in Treasury bonds and bank scrip.

- Leads militia of 13,000 troops to Pennsylvania to suppress Whiskey Rebellion against federal liquor tax.

This record of accomplishment at a time of great uncertainty and turbulence has never again been equaled. It should also give us confidence as to just how much can be done in a time of crisis, if decisive action is taken. In my opinion, the partnership of Washington and Hamilton was absolutely critical to putting America on the path of economic growth and security. Upon Secretary Hamilton's resignation in early 1795, President Washington honored him with these words: "In every relation which you have borne to me, I have found that my confidence in your talents, exertions, and integrity has been well placed."

When President Washington was called to his final summons just before Christmas in 1799, Hamilton responded in kind: "He was an aegis [protector] very essential to me."

Both George Washington and Alexander Hamilton were self-reliant men who took responsibility not only for their own lives but for their country as well. They took the initiative and were alert to opportunities, undaunted by huge challenges, and had confidence in themselves and their country. They were continually confronted with long odds to achieve success and responded, "Why not?" George Washington had never commanded more than a regiment before assuming command of the Continental Army. Alexander Hamilton was a complete unknown when he landed on America's shores, but within five years, he was serving as General Washington's chief of staff.

• *An Engine that Would Not Rest*

These stories of America's Founding Fathers were an inspiration to another man of humble beginnings and an ambition, "like an engine that would not rest," according to his law partner William Herndon.

Abraham Lincoln, our first Republican president, knew firsthand the trials and tribulations of life. His mother died when he was just nine years old, and his illiterate father had no patience with his bookish ways. Even though he had but two years of schooling, he became a well-respected and successful lawyer. He lost both a brother and sister and both of his children as well. Politically, he lost one congressional race and two bids for the U.S. Senate. Shakespeare and the Bible were his constant traveling companions, and he read by candlelight far into the night while his colleagues slumbered.

He formed his economic and political philosophy on the frontier through the careful study of human nature. He was a keen student of our nation's founding documents and "never had a thought politically that did not spring from the sentiments embodied in the Declaration of Independence." The message that all men are created equal was "applicable to all men and all times" and that "advancement, improvement in condition is the order of things in a society of equals."

Lincoln was interested in building a country and society that "allow[ed] the humblest man an equal chance to get rich with everybody else"

Lincoln's thinking never strayed far from our Founding Fathers but he recognized that "we must think anew and act anew."

and left "each man free to acquire property as fast as he can." He had empathy for those who struggled in life but accepted that not all would be successful each time they tried, and that a healthy society accepted the notion that outcomes would be unequal. When his general store in Salem, Illinois, went bust, he paid off his obligations, which he referred to playfully as his "national debt."

He was skeptical of the so-called "levelers," looking to government to ensure more equal results. This was reflected in his view of the proper role of government, as summarized in his 1861 Fourth of July call for:

> a government whose leading object is to elevate the condition of men—to lift artificial weights from all shoulders—to clear the paths of laudable pursuit for all—to afford all an unfettered start and a fair chance in the race of life.

President Lincoln's life embodied the values of frontier self-reliance and independence, compassion, hard work, a sense of humor, and lifelong learning as he persevered through failure and disappointment to become a leading lawyer and perhaps our greatest president.

As we celebrate Lincoln's 200th birthday, let us keep his life and lessons in mind as we face our current troubles. While he had a well-formed conservative philosophy, he remained humble and flexible, believing that "the dogmas of the quiet past are inadequate to the stormy present." Lincoln's thinking never strayed far from our Founding Fathers but he recognized that "we must think anew and act anew."

Lincoln was a firm believer in fostering economic opportunity and innovation. He helped create a culture of invention in America. One of Lincoln's stump speeches as he explored a run for the presidency was entitled, "Discoveries and Inventions". In it, he said "We here in America think we discover, and invent, and improve, faster than any (European nation)." A steady stream of inventors passed through his White House, and he is the only president with a U.S. patent (for a device to lift boats over sandbars). He also signed the Homestead Act in 1862, which allowed citizens to acquire and develop 160 acres of land, leading to the settling of 270 million acres on the western frontier.

Finally, Abraham Lincoln's ambition, the fuel that drove his mighty engine, was the mission of serving his country. In 1850, Lincoln told his law partner, "How hard, oh how hard it is to die and leave one's country no better than if one had never lived."

President Lincoln also recognized the value of faith as he faced the challenge of holding the Union together, stating, "Without the assistance of the Divine Being, I cannot succeed. With that assistance, I cannot fail."

Going Forward with a "Why Not?" Agenda

To renew American prosperity and global leadership, we need a strategy that couples fiscal discipline with robust economic growth. This means an open economy that welcomes legal immigration, tax simplification to unleash American innovation and risk taking, less regulation to help small businesses thrive, and an export boom based on growing with emerging market countries. To reduce spending as the economy grows, we need to prevent Congress from continually "kicking the can down the road". The President needs to declare a "fiscal emergency" setting the stage for legislation that imposes fiscal discipline.

Can we capture the values, attitudes, and spirit of Washington, Hamilton, and Lincoln as we face today's challenges and opportunities? It really comes down to asking the right questions. Asking the big questions that will generate big improvements. What could America look like in 2020 or 2030 if together we do the following:

- Put in place the simplest, most growth-oriented tax system in the world. Why not?

- Pay off our national debt in thirty years by putting 2 percent of the simple tax revenue into a debt reduction fund. Why not?

- Increase the high school graduation rate to 90 percent, making America the world leader in educational opportunity and achievement. Why not?

- Conserve and protect our natural resources while America becomes a net energy exporter through electrifying the grid and expanding clean power. Why not?

- End all distinctions among Americans based on ethnicity, class, or religion. Why not?

- Double American contributions to charitable causes and organizations over the next decade. Why not?

- Achieve a sustained 5 percent economic growth rate by doubling American exports over the next decade, growing with emerging markets, opening new markets through bilateral commercial agreements with major trading partners, and expanding manufacturing at home. Why not?

- Make America the healthiest country in the world by Americans taking more personal responsibility for their health and leading a global initiative to cure chronic disease rather than just treat it. Why not?

- Help entrepreneurs and small businesses create jobs and wealth by eliminating taxes on new ventures during their first five years and cutting the capital gains tax to zero to encourage investment and risk taking.

- Unleash the talents of America's baby boomers as they near and reach traditional retirement age. Why not?

With the right policies, American senior citizens can spark a spike in American innovation and entrepreneurship, as the sixty-five-plus age bracket in America grows from 35 million in 2000 to 72 million in 2030, accounting for 20 percent of America's population. Spurred on by bruised nest eggs and zero taxation on the first $50,000 of income (indexed to inflation), senior citizens will supercharge our economy while volunteering in droves to support charitable causes.

Paying off the national debt in thirty years is doable.

At the time of our nation's birth, our debt relative to our economy was staggering. Nonetheless, Treasury Secretary Alexander Hamilton developed a plan to pay it off in thirty years. It took a bit longer, but under President Andrew Jackson, who stood tall in the Oval Office despite a bullet lodged in his chest, the debt side of America's ledger was wiped clean.

In 1946, after enormous increases in borrowing to pay for

World War II, the national debt equaled 122 percent of GDP. With strong economic growth and lower spending, this was brought down to 33 percent of GDP by 1982. Unfortunately, the upward trend in spending resumed, and our national debt is now roughly 80 percent of GDP. At all costs, we must avoid the fate of Japan, which, due to a series of ten spending stimulus packages after its own banking and real estate meltdown, brought its public debt to an unmanageable 180 percent of its economic output.

America is spending about $2 trillion a year on health care, and it is escalating at the alarming rate of 9 percent per year. If we just continue to primarily treat the symptoms of health problems with prescription drugs, demographic trends in America will force expenditures to explode along with the government budget that covers most of these costs for seniors. In short, if nothing is done differently and current cost and budget trends continue, America risks becoming an economic basket case.

> What if, instead of just treating diseases, we focused our resources and efforts on breakthroughs that cure diseases, such as diabetes?

But what if, instead of just treating diseases, we focused our resources and efforts on breakthroughs that cure diseases, such as diabetes? For every cure, the budget savings to consumers and the government would be enormous. This is not the business model of big pharmaceutical companies but, rather, the purview of smaller, more entrepreneurial biotechnology firms. Many will fail but the few that succeed will do so on a spectacular scale.

A Time to Dare and Endure

America has never been a society driven by class resentment. Yet the current budget is predicated on a class divide. The president issued a pledge that no new burdens will fall on 95 percent of the American people. All the costs will be borne by the rich, and all benefits redistributed downward. But the top 5 percent of income earners already account for 62 percent of federal tax revenue, and the top 20 percent account for more than 90 percent of tax revenue.

The United States has always thrived as a decentralized nation and is skeptical, even scornful, of top-down planning. Yet the current administration is rapidly consolidating power in Washington. America is at its best when state and local governments and organizations such as charities have the upper hand.

America has traditionally at least tried to curtail the growth of the central government. But federal spending as a share of GDP is likely to surpass that of socialist Europe, and that will mean less opportunity and lower possibilities for millions of Americans. Even columnist Roger Cohen, normally a cheerleader for the new administration, seems uncomfortable with the scope and speed of the country's new path:

> Still, the $3.6 trillion Obama budget made me a little queasy. There is a touch of France in its *étatisme*—

the state as all-embracing solution rather than problem—and there's more than a touch of France in the bash-the-rich righteousness with which the new president cast his plans as "a threat to the status quo in Washington."

The question is, what path will America take in the midst of this deep economic downturn? Will it choose the easy way of stimulating the economy with a flood of dollars without regard of the long-term catastrophic consequences? Will it stay true to ideals and principles that made America the envy of the world? Will we return to the failed policies of the 1970s? This was a time that Paul Johnson refers to as America's lost decade and America's suicide attempt.

It is time to choose our nation's future. What America will look like in 2020 will be directly attributable to the choices we make today.

Though challenging, the choices we face today are no more daunting than those that faced George Washington and Alexander Hamilton at the birth of our nation, the passions that almost ripped our country asunder that confronted President Lincoln, or the series of financial panics we surmounted during the nineteenth century and the trauma of the Great Depression during the American century.

> *"This no time for ease and comfort. It is the time to dare and endure. "*
>
> —Sir Winton Churchill

America is too great a country to think and act small even

in the most challenging times. As Adlai Stevenson once said, "America is a country that can gag on a gnat but swallow tigers whole."

In 1931, as the Depression was taking root, the cornerstone of the Empire State Building was laid, and it was completed in only fourteen months (that's 4.5 stories per week!). It was financed privately at a total cost of $41 million. On the other side of the continent, the magnificent marvel of the Golden Gate Bridge was built thanks to a $35 million bond offering approved by voters in 1931. Historian David McCullough, in his epic story of the building of the Brooklyn Bridge, describes the financial panic of 1873, when the most famous banking firm of the day, Jay Cooke & Company, went bankrupt and thousands of businesses went bust.

Despite several years of economic setbacks, the country still moved ahead, propelled by an inextinguishable momentum and enthusiasm.

Our future is in our hands. But our hands must be strong, nimble, and confident, for history shows that great countries and civilizations often fail due to one or more of three shortcomings: a lack of fiscal discipline; a culture that does not promote risk taking, openness, scientific innovation, or the common good; and a foreign policy not grounded in the national interest and executed at the extremes of isolationism or foreign interventionism.

Mark Twain wrote *Huckleberry Finn*. Andrew Carnegie built

the largest steel mill in the world, and railroads tied the country together in one vast network. Thomas Edison invented the electric light bulb. The nation's longest tunnel and tallest building were completed.

Economic downturns frequently are seen as periods of opportunity for entrepreneurs. Microsoft, Genentech, The Gap, and The Limited were all founded during recessions. Hewlett-Packard, Geophysical Service (now Texas Instruments), United Technologies, Polaroid, and Revlon started in the Depression.

As James Baldwin put it, "Those who say it can't be done are usually interrupted by others doing it." Oftentimes, perfect is the enemy of good, and as General George S. Patton put it, "A good plan, executed now, is better than a perfect plan executed next week."

Our future is in our hands.

But our hands must be strong, nimble, and confident, for history shows that great countries and civilizations often fail due to one or more of three shortcomings: a lack of fiscal discipline; a culture that does not promote risk taking, openness, scientific innovation, or the common good; and a foreign policy not grounded in the national interest and executed at the extremes of isolationism or foreign interventionism.

Our confidence in America's future is based on our country's strengths and its proven ability to weather tough times. Peggy Noonan in *Patriotic Grace* closes with a hopeful message about America's resiliency:

Great countries can take a lot of punishment and recover from a lot of loss.... We are a great nation populated by a gifted and still-gritty people. We have deep spiritual resources, a sturdy system of laws, enduring traditions of generosity and support, and military and technical prowess and might.

America is a great and good country. Let's make it even greater and better. All we need to do is to renew our commitment to the traits that created the American century: liberty and self-reliance, mobility and opportunity, innovation and technology, investment and growth, organization and management, and flexibility and scale. This will not only benefit America, for as Ronald Reagan put it in his farewell speech from the Oval Office:

"We meant to change a nation, and instead, we changed a world."

Bibliography

Dean Acheson, *Present at the Creation: My Years in the State Department*, W.W. Norton and Company, 1969.

David Aikman. *Jesus in Beijing: How Christianity is Changing China and the Global Balance of Power.* Regnery, 2003.

Andrew Bacevich. *The Limits of Power: The End of American Exceptionalism.* Metropolitan Books, 2008.

William J. Bennett. *America: The Last Best Hope.* Nelson Current, 2006.

Bradley Project on America's National Identity. "E Pluribus Unum." June 2008.

Douglas Brinkley. *The Wilderness Warrior: Theodore Roosevelt and the Crusade for America.* HarperCollins, 2009.

James McGregor Burns. *The Vineyard of Liberty.* Alfred A. Knopf, 1982.

Gwyneth Cravens. *Power to Change the World: The Truth About Nuclear Energy.* Vintage, 2008.

Ron Chernow. *Alexander Hamilton.* Penguin Press, 2004.

G. K. Chesterton. "What is America?" in *What I Saw in America.* Da Capo Press, 1968._

Amy Chua. *Day of Empire.* Doubleday, 2007.

Sir Winston Churchill (Edited by Winston S. Churchill). *The Great Republic.* Random House, 2000.

Sir Winston Churchill. *History of the English-Speaking Peoples.* Dorset (reissue edition), 1990.

Sir Winston Churchill. "If I Were an American," in *Life.* April 14, 1947.

Sir Winston Churchill. *My Early Life.* Charles Scribner's Sons, 1930.

William J. Clinton, *Giving: How Each of Us Can Change the World*, Alfred A. Knopf, 2007.

Alistair Cook, *Reporting America*, The Overlook Press, 2008.

Hernando De Soto. *The Mystery of Capital: Why Capitalism Triumphs in the West and Fails Everywhere Else.* Basic Books, 2000.

Dinesh D'Souza. "What's Great about America," First Principles Series #1. Washington, DC: The Heritage Foundation, 2006.

Anthony Faiola. "China Worried About U.S. Debt," in *The Washington Post.* March 14, 2009.

Benjamin Friedman, *The Moral Consequences of Economic Growth*, Knopf, 2005.

Barry Goldwater. *The Conscience of a Conservative.* Victor Publishing, 1960.

John Steele Gordon. *Empire of Wealth: The Epic History of American Economic Power.* Random House, 2009.

David Halberstam. *The Coldest Winter: America and the Korean War.* Hyperion, 2007.

David Halberstam. *The Next Century.* William Morrow Company, 1991.

Alexander Hamilton, et al. "The Federalist Papers," No. 10, No. 51.

Victor Davis Hanson. *Mexifornia: A State of Becoming.* Encounter Books, 2007.

Stephen Haseler. *Super-State, The New Europe and its Challenge to America.* St. Martin's Press, 2004.

Walter Isaacson and Evan Thomas, *The Wise Men: Six Friends and the World They Made*, Simon & Schuster, 1987.

Robert Kagan. *The Return of History.* Alfred A. Knopf, 2008.

Parag Khanna. *The Second World: Empires and Influence in the New Global Order.* Random House, 2008.

Kishore Mahbubani. "The New Asian Hemisphere: The Irresistible Shift of Global Power to the East," in *Public Affairs*, 2008.

Thomas F. Madden, *Empire of Trust*, Penguin Group, 2008.

David McCullough. *The Great Bridge: The Epic Story of Building the Brooklyn Bridge.* Simon & Schuster, 1972.

Hans J. Morgenthau. "Politics Amongst Nations: The Struggle for Peace and Power," McGraw-Hill Companies,1948.

Nandan Nilekani. *Imagining India: The Idea of a Renewed India.* Penguin Press, 2009.

Peggy Noonan. *Patriotic Grace: What it Is and Why We Need it Now.* HarperCollins, 2008.

Grover Norquist. *Leave Us Alone.* HarperCollins, 2008.

Office of the U.S. Secretary of Defense. "Military Power of the People's Republic of China 2009," A Report to Congress Pursuant to the National Defense Authorization Act of 2000, 2009.

Kevin Phillips. *Wealth and Democracy.* Broadway Books, 2002.

David S. Reynolds. *Waking Giant: America in the Age of Jackson.* HarperCollins, 2008.

Theodore Roosevelt. *Theodore Roosevelt: An Autobiography.* Macmillan, 1913.

David Sanger. *The Inheritance.* Harmony Books, 2009.

Arthur M. Schlesinger, Jr. *The Disuniting of America: Reflections on a Multicultural Society.* W.W. Norton, 1998.

Brent Scowcroft and Zbignew Brezenski. *America and the World.* Basic Books, 2008.

Kiron K. Skinner, Annelise Anderson, and Martin Anderson. *Reagan in His Own Hand.* The Free Press, 2001.

David Smick. *The World Is Curved.* Penguin Books, 2008.

Rodney Stark. *The Victory of Reason: How Christianity Led to Freedom, Capitalism, and Western Success.* Random House, 2005.

Irwin Stelzer. *The New Capitalism.* Hudson Institute, 2008.

Mark Steyn. *America Alone.* Regnery Publishing, 2006.

Margaret Thatcher. *Margaret Thatcher: The Downing Street Years.* HarperCollins, 1993.

Barbara W. Tuchman. *The March of Folly.* Michael Joseph London, 1984.

Sun Tzu (Edited by James Clavell). *The Art of War.* Dell Publishing, 1983.

U.S. News & World Report. "The State of America's Health in 2009," February 2009.

Karel Van Wolferen. *The Enigma of Japanese Power.* Knopf, 1989.

Carl von Clausewitz. "On War." Princeton, N.J., Wilder Publications, 2008.

George Washington. "Farewell Address." September 19, 1797.

Ronald C. White, Jr. *A. Lincoln.* Random House, 2009.

Jay Winik. *The Great Upheaval: America and the Birth of the Modern World.* HarperCollins, 2007.

Gordon S. Wood. *Revolutionary Characters.* Penguin Press, 2006.

Walter B. Wriston. *Risk & Other Four-Letter Words.* Harper & Row, 1986.

About the Author

Carl Delfeld is head of the financial publishing firm Chartwell ETF and the investment advisory firm Chartwell Partners. He writes the "Global Gambits" column for *Forbes Asia*, is the author of four books on global investing, and is chairman of the economic strategy think tank America Unbound.

Carl served on the executive board of directors of the Asian Development Bank in Manila during the administration of George H. W. Bush and, as a vice president with Robert W. Baird & Company, opened markets in Tokyo, Hong Kong, and Australia.

He served on the staff of Senator William V. Roth, author of the 1981 tax cuts and sponsor of the Roth IRA, on the Joint Economic Committee and the U.S. Senate Finance Committee, was a consultant to the U.S. Treasury, and was a member of the U.S.-Pacific Economic Cooperation Committee. He is a graduate of the Fletcher School of Law & Diplomacy and studied at Harvard University's Asia Center as well as at Sophia University and Keio University in Tokyo, Japan.

Carl lives in Colorado with his wife Marilou and children Jackie and Robert. He can be reached at cdelfeld@mac.com or (719) 264-1503.

About the America Unbound Foundation

America Unbound is an economic strategy non-profit organization that promotes pro-growth policies, monitors developments in China and encourages closer economic and political ties with emerging market countries.

Akin to a venture capitalist, we work with like-minded experts and organizations with a bias on action rather than long policy reports.

Our Center for Economic Diplomacy encourages business executives and especially entrepreneurs to get more involved in emerging markets and helps educate the future leaders of American economic diplomacy.

For more information or to contribute to America Unbound, please go to AmericaUnbound.org or call 719.264.1503